FOR CHICKS ONLY

5,000
Reasons to Smile...
for Chicks

SANTA MONICA PRESS

SALLY DeLELLIS

Copyright ©2005 by Sally DeLellis

All rights reserved. This book may not be reproduced in whole or in part or in any form or format without written permission of the publisher.

Published by:

SANTA MONICA PRESS

Santa Monica Press LLC
P.O. Box 1076
Santa Monica, CA 90406-1076
1-800-784-9553
www.santamonicapress.com
books@santamonicapress.com

Printed in the United States

Santa Monica Press books are available at special quantity discounts when purchased in bulk by corporations, organizations, or groups. Please call our Special Sales Department at 1-800-784-9553.

Library of Congress Cataloging-in-Publication Data

DeLellis, Sally, 1975-
  5,000 reasons to smile-- for chicks / by Sally DeLellis.
     p. cm.
  ISBN 1-59580-002-6
 1. Conduct of life--Humor. I. Title: Five thousand reasons to smile--
for chicks. II. Title.
  PN6231.C6142D46 2005
  818'.602--dc22
                                        2005009521

Cover and interior design by Future Studio

For Ava, my chick-in-training

and

John, who always makes me smile

Your own cooking

A witty joke

Because you went to an Ivy League school

Your nieces and nephews

Your first apartment

A good day

A good new beer

A flattering photo

A cute notepad

Chocolate-covered pretzels

Heart-shaped Post-it notes

Finding a few dollars in last winter's coat

Your letter to the editor getting published

VCR/DVD combos

Acing the GRE

Adding extra reps to your set

Quitting smoking for good

You're healthy, happy, and hip

Breast petals

Pilates' effects on your psyche
(not to mention abs)!

Your skinny jeans

Autumn nights

The smell of burning leaves

Memories of playing Chinese jump rope

Recalling the baby powder scent
of your Cabbage Patch Kids

Sweet dreams

Sexy dreams

A tearjerker movie

The times you've made the first move

Tees with built-in bras

The fad you loved at 13 is back in style

Seaweed body wraps

The smell of chlorine on a hot August day

Free night and weekend minutes

Cooking your first Thanksgiving turkey

Ribbed turtlenecks

Clearance racks

Frequent buyer clubs

Going through old photos

The hot new guy at work

Stores with a price adjustment policy

Making a new friend

Courteous drivers

Christmas club checks

When a young person turns to you for advice

People who say "thank you" and mean it

Compliments on your cooking

Reigniting a romance

Adding "in bed" to your fortune cookie's fortune

Renewing a friendship

Birthday cards in the mail

Victoria's Secret panties

Nick and Nora flannel pajamas

An unexpected promotion

Good advice

Reading the Sunday paper

A winning scratch-off lottery ticket

Being two pounds thinner at your weigh-in than you expected

A completed to-do list

Sleeping in

Memories of past hangovers

New magazines

Comfy denim jackets

Boots with a heel

Looking forward to your therapy appointment

Pizza with meatballs and garlic

The smell of Christmas trees

Low-rise thongs

Animal print pocket tissues

A job well done

Knowing you took the high road

An invitation

A genuine compliment

Art deco martini glasses

A new drink

Trying a new food and liking it

A great idea

Football games on Sunday

Chinese takeout

Earning a graduate degree

A facial at Bliss Spa

Rereading Judy Blume's
Are You There, God? It's Me, Margaret.

Watching *Saved By the Bell* reruns
when you're home sick

Spotting a celebrity

You're a bold Aries chick

A new sushi restaurant opening in your neighborhood

The Find and Replace features in Microsoft Word

Letting go of a grudge

Forgiving someone

Stars to wish upon

Colored cell phone covers

Handbag addictions

The cherry aroma of Chianti

Going to a baseball game in June

Charm bracelets

The confidence you never had in your teens

Las Vegas

Sick days

Your ten year high school reunion

Snow days

Gift cards to your favorite store

New releases at the video store

Day spas

Running a 5K

Vermont Teddy Bears for no reason

Whole wheat pancakes

Apartments that take pets

Cubic zirconium

Home Depot's Do-It-Herself Workshops

Hallmark's free date books

Eyelash curlers

Sterling silver Tiffany bracelets

Crystal tattoos

Waterproof mascara

Phone scams on your morning radio show

UV-free tanning salons

Being fabulous

The goofy things you used to do with your best friend in seventh grade

Permanent French manicures

Fruit-flavored water

Jeans with stretch

Closet exchange parties with your girlfriends

Sunday brunch at a trendy restaurant with your friends

Because you're not too old
to dress up for Halloween

Canceled meetings

Because 40 is the new 30

Because 30 is still considered a kid

Because you can keep a secret

Window shopping on eluxury.com

A new novel by your favorite author

A flapper dress

A great haircut

No traffic

Your awkward teen years are over

Monogrammed everything

The prank calls you used to make

Edy's Dreamery ice cream

Fake belly rings

Reruns of *Dallas* on SOAPnet

VH1's *I Love the '80s*

Picturing your name in lights

Going to a surprise 40th birthday party

Shimmery body lotion

Burberry plaid

Nancy Ganz body slimmers

Clip-on ponytails

Spinning classes

Frizz fighting hair serums

Green tea

Olive oil to touch up your nails

Movie versions of TV shows you loved as a kid

Healthy choices at fast food restaurants

Thong panty liners

All girl get-togethers

The revival of fondue parties

Lavender candles

Funky cosmetic cases

Frequent-flyer miles

Water resistant cell phones

Sheer nail polish

Heart-shaped nail polish remover pads

Leather pants

Suede miniskirts

Younger men

When the sweater you love
rings up less than marked

Madonna's old music

MP3 players

Palm pilots

Your non-intrusive landlord

Desserts by mail

Seeing "The Boss" in concert

French bulletin boards

Rereading your old Nancy Drew books

Your whole life being ahead of you

Cashmere gloves

Faux fur

Your first mortgage

Personal pizzas

You're a creative Pisces chick

Brazilian bikini waxes

Cosmopolitans

Thongs

Cheesecake-of-the-month clubs

Having a queen bed all to yourself

IM-ing five people at once

Daily horoscopes delivered to your inbox

Sex and the City DVDs

Flavored vodkas

Made-for-TV movies

Appletinis

First kisses

Low mortgage rates

Being self-sufficient

Last-minute cheap vacations

Having your own secretary

Road trips

Beach houses

Online shopping

A swing coat

Flirting without guilt

Friends of the opposite sex

Total control of the remote

Eating the same thing for dinner
five days in a row

Online matchmakers
with free membership for women

Godiva chocolates

Iced coffee

One-day sales

Baseball games on TV every day
from April to October

Outdoor concerts

Anticipation before the first date

Flattering fitting room mirrors

Glamour magazine

Older men

Shopping at Wal-Mart

Happy hour specials

2-for-1 appetizers

The Louis Vuitton Accessory Pouch

Bachelorette parties

Jean jackets from The Gap

Bargains on eBay

The Jeep Liberty

Drinking your glass of Rosé
with an ice cube

A subscription to a Wine-of-the-Month club

Abs crunches

A session with a personal trainer

The scent of Citre Shine shampoo

Buying yourself flowers

Buttercream-scented candles

Pre-ordering your movie tickets on the Internet

Vanilla-scented linen spray

Holding the winning ticket at a raffle

Yankee Candle's Sage Citrus scent

A feather boa on New Year's Eve

A rhinestone horseshoe necklace

Your hideous junior high hairstyle

The New York, NY casino in Vegas

Going to Cancun with your girlfriends

400 thread count sheets

iTunes

A silk kimono

www.mypoints.com

Your stylist understanding you

The thrill of reading Judy Blume's *Forever* as an adolescent

Thigh highs

You're a dependable Capricorn chick

Taylor ham, egg, and cheese on a hard roll at 2 A.M.

Feng shui

Suntan lotion's coconut scent

Buy one, get one free anything

New Year's Eve in Times Square

Online bill pay

No roommate

Friends you can cry openly in front of during movies

Your birthstone is peridot

A clear conscience

An iPod for your birthday

Surviving a broken heart

Your job is fulfilling

Cell phones with a camera

The pink ribbon on your lapel

Learning something each day

Alone time

Happy childhood memories

Your first business card

A raise

A holiday bonus at work

A good luck charm that works

Icons in your IM's

Your favorite song is on the radio

www.women.com

A Tiffany and Co. purse pen

Clothes that don't require dry cleaning

Magnets on your fridge

Renting a limo for a night out

A mother who is also a friend

A sizzling goodnight kiss

Sending Valentines
to all of your unattached friends

Fireworks on July 4th

Online purity tests

A cute key chain

A souvenir from a memorable vacation

Melrose Place reruns on the Style channel

A winning bid on eBay

Your eyes are the color of turquoise

Pralines in a salad

Singing in the car

Clever puns

Black pants

Keeping your houseplants alive

Shopgirl by Steve Martin

A subscription to *Marie Claire*

Your birth flower is the carnation (January)

Getting checked out
when you're not feeling pretty

Skinny Cow ice cream sandwiches

Cinematherapy by Beverly West and Nancy Peske

Meeting with a financial planner

A boatneck tee

Big sweaters

Casual Fridays

A gold nameplate necklace

Cleaning out your junk drawer

A perfectly wrapped gift

The first of your friends is pregnant

Jalapeño poppers

Remembering your monthly breast exam

Visiting the Rock and Roll Hall of Fame

Relaxing on your patio

A pixie haircut

'80s music

A celebrity crush

Miniature *For Dummies* books

The speed of cable modems

Making a scrapbook

Playing bunko

The condoms in your purse

Keeping New Year's resolutions

A refund from the IRS

Bloomingdale's Big Brown Bag

The end of a semester

A company picnic

Labrador retriever puppies

Pictures with friends

Chocolate-covered strawberries

Nike sneakers

Taking a Carnival Cruise

Getting a massage in Disney's Grand Floridian Spa

The Mercedes C240

Midol PMS

Keeping your options open

Funky mousepads

Topless beaches

A second date

You're a Libra chick who likes to keep the peace

Telling the truth when you'd rather not

More shoes than you need

Swarovski's Little Red Dress pin

A killer presentation

Knowing the answers on *Jeopardy!*

Drinking a hurricane at a tiki bar

Days when you're just not that hungry

Loft parties

Cosmetic wedges

Free memory upgrades

Party buses

Dating two guys

Taking a risk

A leather sofa

An organic diet

Sam Adams Chocolate Bock

Palm trees

Super Bowl Sunday

Conversation hearts

Well-behaved children in public places

A racy joke

Old Navy $5 tees

Horizontal stripes

Your own office

Gum whose flavor lasts

The crazy stunts you got away with as a kid

The crazy stunts you didn't get away with as a kid

The *90210* prom episode

Text messaging

Flatscreen computer monitors

Relaxing in a hot tub

A cheesy pick-up line

Following your heart

Noxzema

Having curves

A Chihuahua that fits in your purse

Putting away some extra money

Tiffany blue

Eating lunch in the park

Defending your dissertation
A string of pearls
White roses
Finding new pals
A Bellini with thick peach wedges
Elliptical trainer machines
A bargain from IKEA
Warehouse sales
World Vegetarian Day (October 1)
Paying off your student loans
Apple cider vinegar in your bath water
Wonder Woman
Spam filters in your e-mail
Carrie's naked dress
A sizzling summer
Abstinence by choice
A dream dictionary
Wine tasting dinners
Asymmetrical hems
Saying you're sorry
Passing the NCLEX with flying colors

Umbrellas in frozen drinks

No cavities

Showing skin

Bad boys

Checks with a cute design

Coach wristlets

Decorative notebooks

Clever haiku

Paid overtime

Entering a contest

Winning a contest

Cookie mixes that taste like scratch

Making a difficult decision

A yoga regimen

Visiting Europe for the first time

Getting a new puppy or kitten

Quick dry nail polish

Lucy Van Pelt's take-no-crap attitude

Cinco de Mayo

Trying a new position

Looking good naked

Paying your Visa in full every month

Sleeping with the lights on

Having a tampon when you need one

Secret Santa gifts

Fajitas and 'ritas

Participating in a breast cancer walk

Sunning in the Hamptons

Moving into a new place

Horoscope-a-day calendars

Chopping your hair off

Matchbox 20 in concert

Putting on a black shirt without getting deodorant on it

Thursday nights

You're an honest Sagittarius chick

Memories of your first period

Sending *him* flowers

Trusting your instincts

Sequins

Liberal return policies

Your first godchild

A box of wine

Losing 5 pounds in a month

Going to New Orleans during Mardi Gras

A chilled glass

What braces did for your teeth

Free downloads

Male revues

Hitting the ski slopes

Doing someone a favor

Messenger bags

Mini-fishnet pantyhose

An expense account

Friday the 13th

Leaving a great tip

Metallic lace

A newsboy cap

Overnight shipping

Strawberry Shortcake coming back into style

Brie cheese baked with brown sugar

Rollerblading through the park

Getting over a cold

Your plane departating on time

Brightly colored sand in glass jars
Not gaining the Freshman 15
Watching cartoon reruns
A true crime book
The national Do Not Call list
Wine collecting
Your best friend's wedding day
Karaoke bars
Multiple orgasms
A feeling of déjà vu
An exciting offer
Internet coupons
Tankinis
Gabbing on the phone
Your parents' anniversary
Drinking a Shirley Temple
Free beaches at the Jersey Shore
The Rainforest Cafe
Leopard print pillows
Perfect posture
Cooking101 on cookinglight.com

Pumpkin picking in the fall

A handsome stranger

Making a donation

No annual fees

18k gold

Changing careers

High heels with ankle straps

Paella and a pitcher of sangria

Regular pap smears

Partying in Key West

A convertible VW beetle

Capri pants

Lord and Taylor savings passes

Making a new contact

Buying a cute baby gift

Clean public restrooms

Home dry cleaning kits

Women's History Month (March)

Champagne flutes
with Swarovski crystal-filled stems

Biore pore cleanser

Dr. Scholl's slides

Spa Finder magazine

Dean Koontz novels

The office gossip

Scoring free drinks

A fundraising dinner

You're a Taurus chick who loves being pampered

A serious romance

Keeping your mouth shut at the right time

Everything in moderation

Baseball caps and ponytails

Your company AmEx card

Custom-fit swimsuits

Bubblegum greeting cards

No lines for the fitting room

A Long Beach Iced Tea

Antiques at flea markets

CK's Sheer Obsession

Early episodes of *Sex and the City* when Carrie was with Big

Listening to a book on CD in the car

Empty malls in January

A fresh start

Pom

Tickets to *Cirque du Soleil*

An aromatherapy sound machine

Tricep kickbacks

Invisible deodorant

Going on a double date

Harlequin's *Flipside* series

The birth control patch

A scarf tied around your wrist

Great gifts under $50

Gossiping by the water cooler

Squelching a rumor

Taking a catnap

Victoria's Secret scented bra sachets

Neutral lip liner

Teeth whitening strips

Paraffin manicures

A good kisser

A massaging footbath

Bumping into your ex when you look great

Walking around your apartment in your underwear

Sephora stores

Cosmpolitan's "Guy Without His Shirt"

Irish coffee

Seeing *Mamma Mia* on Broadway

Sleep masks

Relaxing on a chaise lounge

Playing Uno

Steamed asparagus à la carte

Recommending a restaurant you love to someone

Finding the perfect greeting card

A commendation from your boss

Liking what you see when you look in the mirror

Not getting up to catch the bouquet at a wedding

Bloody Marys at breakfast

A leather blazer

A kiss hello

Flat-screen TVs

Zip drives

A friend who would never betray you

Track pants

Boy short panties

The pins and needles feeling in your legs after a great workout

Craig the cheerleader on *Saturday Night Live*

Cheating on your diet once in a while

Picking up shells on the beach

Hand blown wine glasses

Pay-per-view concerts

Spell check on Word

Playing Truth or Dare as a grownup

Concierge-level hotel rooms

Mood lipstick just for fun

Making out

A freshly made bed

Russell Stover Valentine hearts

Legally Blonde

Corduroy pants

Coach sneakers

Getting published

Designated drivers

Setting your clocks back

Making a decadent dessert from
The Cake Mix Doctor

An hour-long kickboxing class

St. Gennaro's feast in Little Italy

You know what "tea length" is

Getting the restaurant's best table

Being in the spotlight

Taking self-help books with a grain of salt

Twizzlers

Trinket boxes

Hoop earrings

Cleavage

Voice-activated dialing

Monopoly deeds

Good news

Cajun martinis

Twinkies

The Awakening by Kate Chopin

Shearling earmuffs

Tiffany Etoile jewelry

The first day of spring

A perfectly full moon

Talking about Santa to a child who still believes

Attending a movie premiere

Smooth legs

Moving out of your parents' house

Dive bars

You're an organized Virgo chick

Irish pubs

Sexy eyeglasses

Multicolored leis

The drunken dialing you did
in your early 20s

Photo storage boxes

Exercising your right to choose

Declining an invitation
when you just don't feel like going

Waking up to a blanket of snow

Venetian glass jewelry

"Standing Still" by Jewel

Makeup samples

Reflexology massage

Avon lip gloss cards

Rose-tinted sunglasses

Clinique's free gift with purchase
A straw bag for summer
Extended shopping hours
Company holiday parties
Quiet evenings
A call from a long-lost friend
M & M ColorWorks
A relaxing weekend at a bed and breakfast
Hosting a dinner party
Americangreetings.com
Being your sister's MOH
Taking your sweet time
Gourmet food markets
Not taking "no" for an answer
The Bold and the Beautiful
The smell of leather
Being happy with what you have
Satin sheets
Stormy weekends
Taking a ceramics class
No runs in your pantyhose

Shopping at Banana Republic

A cotton chemise

Querying a magazine

Dancing Queen by Abba

Tag Heuer watches

Sturdy shopping bags

Loafer socks

Taking the stairs instead of the elevator

Hula hooping with your nieces

No wait at the hair salon

A clean driving record

Cajun cheeseburgers

Safe sex

A fantasy vacation

Furniture from Pier 1 Imports

Liz Claiborne fragrances

Miranda and Steve

Baking a cake from scratch for your best friend's birthday

Being a swinging single

Austin Powers' teeth

Volunteering

A canopy bed

Dom Perignon

Saying "yes" instead of "yeah"

An orangey-pink sunset

Sapphire jewelry

Halter tops

Your birth flower is the Violet (February)

CK Easy Fit jeans

Driving a convertible

Price checkers in a department store

Doritos and guacamole

A pleasant surprise

Big Red gum

Laughing so hard you cry

A Dairy Queen Blizzard

Outdoor cafes

The latest issue of *People* magazine

Working from home

An indoor light box to beat the winter blues

The Le Creuset Pepper Pot

You're a spontaneous Gemini chick

Having your heart stolen

Your first solo vacation

Mini camcorders

The Audi A4

A lazy weekend

Going to Culture Club in NYC

Rereading old love letters

Day to night outfits

Falling in love

Hershey's Kisses

Having your book signed by your favorite author

Being good at what you do

Makeup remover

Homemade Valentines

Sampling beers from around the world in Epcot

Princess-cut diamonds

The Joy Luck Club by Amy Tan

Compatible neighbors

Getting measured to find your true bra size

Googling someone

Joining a fan club

Saks Fifth Avenue

Chubby squirrels outside your apartment in the fall

Overstock.com

Louis Vuitton Monogram Vernis

New refills for your agenda

Bangle bracelets

Makeup bags

Organic wine

Placing a personal ad

Blinking lights around your windows

Ignoring the doorbell on Halloween

Vintage clothing

In Style magazine

East Hampton Beach, NY

Being in love

Jazz music

Spending the day in bed

An inside joke

Retro lunch boxes

Muffin tops

The "It's a Small World" ride
in the Magic Kingdom

Feeling inspired

Butterscotch schnapps

Writing a letter

Shave minimizer lotion

Dessert cafes

A scratch and sniff sticker in first grade

Vanilla mint lip balm

A smile from a crush

A reality check

Finding a penny heads up

A clean new notebook

Body glitter

Your lucky number

Sharpie marking pens

Going to the movies every week

Making lists

Going barefoot

Loveseats

Sesame chicken

Riding the Napa Valley Wine Train

A scenic overlook

Dollar Tree stores

Eyebrow grazing bangs

Emoticons

Red pants

Your closet

Pink flamingos

Library book sales

Your hair's natural highlights

Your watch tan line

Exercising your right to vote

Eating frosting with a spoon

A CD player in your shower

'80s glam rock

A summer fling

Leather interior in your car

Your impeccable grammatical skills

Free line dancing lessons
at the local country western bar

The Rising by Bruce Springsteen

Caller ID

Valet parking

Get a Financial Life by Beth Kobliner

Engraved bracelets

Holding hands

One-a-day vitamins

Amazon.com's Listmania

Fresh daisies

Candlelit dinners

A clear and starry night

Push-up bras

Snapple

The smell of fresh laundry

Warm bath towels from the dryer

Ben and Jerry's Half Baked

Because Cancer chicks are homebodies

Being punctual

30 minutes of exercise four times a week

Gaining 5 pounds between Thanksgiving & Christmas and worrying about it after New Year's

Treating a friend

Falling asleep the moment your head hits the pillow

Low-interest student loans

When your boss comes into the office later than you

Ring tunes

Venus razors

Watching *My Big Fat Greek Wedding*

Setting a signature in your e-mail

Popcorn at the movies

Your quest to find the fastest, scariest roller coaster

Having your palms read

Trying on bridesmaids' dresses

Sending an Insta-kiss

Companies with "No Animal Testing" policies

Canvas carryalls from L.L. Bean

Hot chocolate with Kahlua

Visiting the Metropolitan Museum of Art

Daydreams

Breakfast in bed

Estee Lauder's *Pleasures*

Tivo

Setting boundaries

A great parking space

Witty screen names

Random thoughts

The trip to Hawaii you'll take one day

A smile from a stranger

Homemade smoothies

Finding something you thought you lost

An old sweatshirt from your alma mater

Do-it-yourself hair color

After-Christmas clearance

Cheese, bread, and wine

Underneath it All by No Doubt

Cruising along the Pacific Coast Highway

The smell of books

Being in Oprah's studio audience

Playing matchmaker

An annoying coworker got a new job

New $20 bills

National Nurse's Week (early May)

Covered parking

A cliffhanger in your favorite show

A juicy urban legend

Plush slippers

Good credit

Long Beach Island, NJ

When opportunity knocks

Retro sneakers

No fee ATMs

Throwing caution to the wind

Starting your novel

Not being shallow

Early '90s freestyle music

EZ Pass

Catalogs in your mailbox

Coming home after a long day

Going to the city when you're from the country

Going to the country when you're from the city

Thai food

Dancing till dawn

Helping someone without expecting a thing in return

Your birthstone is emerald

Your middle name isn't so bad

Sand between your toes

Static guard

Having a great tailor

Henna tattoos

4-wheel drive

You're handy enough to do most minor household repairs

Memories at the roller rink

Knowing your limits

Bringing in bagels for your friends at work

Finding a chic website

It takes more muscles to frown

Not needing a man to be happy

Your mom's old station wagon

Buying yourself something extravagant

Looking at models of townhomes you couldn't possibly afford

Freshly washed hair

Trying to get in without a reservation

Wine bars

The smell of freshly cut grass

Making your point

A bittersweet moment

Watching your favorite Lifetime TV movie

Hairstyles that don't require an entire can of hair spray

"Stranger in My House" by Tamia

Responding to a personal ad

You're an ambitious Leo chick

Cosmopolitan magazine

Designing your perfect diamond ring online

Seinfeld reruns

Easy to remember PIN numbers

The smell in the air right before a storm

A good stretch in the morning

Your guardian angel

A Cactus Bowl at Houlihan's

A pea coat

Brat Pack movies

Taco salad

Sharing a secret

Putting your worries on hold

A good hair day

Eating with chopsticks

SoapNet

New office furniture

Salt and vinegar potato chips

Your freckles

Your old *Tiger Beat* magazines

Being better off without him

The panic button on your car alarm

Personalized license plates

Bath salts

Wrapping gifts

$1 margaritas between 4 and 6 P.M.

Playing miniature golf

Learning a few phrases in a foreign language

Microstretch Keds

Fashion Week in NYC

Cherry red lipstick

Someone playing with your hair

Urban Decay eye shadow

A much needed hug

An eBay gift certificate

Having an emergency kit in your car

Boot cut jeans

TBS Superstation's "Dinner and a Movie"

Wearing brown
when you want to get down to work

A lazy day

Oprah's Book Club

Psychic moments

A body pillow

Waterbeds

Skinny dipping

Buddy List away messages

A date who opens the door for you

A coffee coolata

Airmall while you're flying

A remote starter in your car

Nine West Jewelry

A Big Mac and fries

Kevyn Aucoin's *Face Forward*

Baby pictures

Sleeping outdoors

Posting a book review on Amazon.com

A hot new fashion designer

Control top pantyhose

Nalgene water bottles

Joining a reading group

The Great American Smokeout

A 10-minute oil change

Smartecarte at the airport

A new mini cooler in a summery color

Mental health days

Homemade macaroni and cheese

A claddagh ring

A left-handed Page-a-Day calendar

Going midnight bowling

Outlet shopping

A perfect eyebrow arch

Cute stickers on your envelopes

Breaking a bad habit

Supersoft sneakers

Lands' End at Sears

Hello Kitty pencils

Full figure bras that are sexy

Brand new sheets

Settling into your newfound singledom

Colorful Images catalogs in the mail

An inspiring quotation

Your parents were right about some things

Jigsaw puzzles

Random happy thoughts

Going horseback riding in the country

All-in-one printers

Your boss is away on a trip

Going camping

Emily Post's *Etiquette*

Administrative Professionals Week (late April)

Adding Kahlua to a chocolate cake mix

The way your car sparkles after a wash

Knowing what you did is for the best

When a child tells you that you're pretty

Buying a shirt you love in every color

Subway sandwiches

You're an open-minded Aquarius chick

Watching old *Love Boat* reruns

A Williams-Sonoma shopping spree

Liking your imperfections

Making things happen

A gripping mystery novel

Watching the *Wizard of Oz* in your pj's

The Florida Keys

Mrs. Field's cookies

Suze Orman's column in *Oprah*

A matinee performance of
The Vagina Monologues

A glass of V8 Splash

Knowing how to change a tire

Cryptograms

The dream kitchen you'll design one day

Throwing a come-as-you-are party

A terry cloth tube top

Forming a supper club

Having the upper hand

Beaded sun catchers

Watching *The First Wives Club*

Chocolate body paint

I.D. bracelets

Pottery Barn furniture

A sweater for your puppy

Not acting your age

Fabrics that forgive your figure flaws

Boyd's Bears

Casting a benevolent spell

Valuing brains over beauty

Your first car

A Jeep Wrangler

A change of heart

Carrot cake petit fours

Azalea bushes

When your inbox is empty

Memories of losing your virginity

Digital voice recorders

A Tiffany & Co. diamond-shaped paperweight

Free guest passes at the gym

Virtual makeover software

Memories of summer camp

Running your fingers through the pink sands of Bermuda

Free web space

A personal motto

Seeing your favorite artist in concert
for the umpteenth time

Colored glass pulls on your kitchen cabinets

Volunteering as a Big Sister

Buying your first piece of art

Bingo at Foxwoods casino

Recommending a movie to a friend

Never looking back

Evening bags shaped like watering cans

New address postcards

Missed meeting passes at Weight Watchers

Your bus is waiting for you

Marquis by Waterford

Taking a stained glass class

Online lists of drinking games

A higher paying position

Feeling safe

Tiny tees

A Wild West party

A PMS-free month

32-pound paper

Laundry service

Green beer on St. Patrick's Day

www.the3day.org

Winning a football pool at work

An overflowing bookcase

Miss Lonelyhearts in *Rear Window*

White chocolate Reese's cups

Wide screen plasma TV's

Rhinestone barrettes

Celebs who aren't stick thin

Metallic makeup

Corset tops

Letting him down easily

Having a respectable CD collection

You're a detail-oriented Scorpio chick

Fancy soaps for guests only

Exercising to beat PMS

Picking a chocolate at random out of a box and it's your favorite flavor

Doing something totally out of character

The weekly Top 40

Circulars in the Sunday paper

Black Russians

Men with chest hair

Returning your videos on time

A street fair in town

Your IQ

A window table

Singing along to "Isn't She Lovely"

The pirate ship ride at amusement parks

Adjuncting at the local community college

When life takes a totally unexpected turn

Pat Benatar's *Best Shots*

Taking a personality test

Being paid a compliment
you've never heard before

Taking a picture with your favorite celebrity
in a wax museum

Visiting your old high school

"I Love You" mini cookie cutters

Knowing you'll try harder next time

Fitness water

Mexican-inspired folk art

A sterling silver ice bucket from Tiffany & Co.

Your greatest accomplishment

Happy lists

A marble frosted Dunkin' Donut

Stocking your home bar

The way you found out there isn't a Santa Claus

A suede coin purse

Q-Tips for beauty emergencies

Camouflage printed lingerie

Not being too proud to ask for help

Speaking your mind

Polka dot bikinis

Sally Hansen Hard As Nails

Saturday Night Live

Lime-flavored nacho chips

Remembering how you used to play "Light as a Feather, Stiff as a Board"

Secretly loving "Mandy" by Barry Manilow

An inspiring memoir

Diet success stories

Swatch watches

Loofah mitts

Flea market finds

Driving a stick shift

H&M bargains

White noise to help you sleep at night

Tea-flavored lollipops

Ball gown skirts

Knowing the proper form of both personal and business letters

Because it's time to party

Ginger Altoids

Embracing your quirks

When your friends love your new boyfriend

Your killer resume

Knowing when to laugh at yourself

Taking life one day at a time

A single red rose

The Mitsubishi Eclipse Spyder

Skin that glows

Online dream groups

Grilled cheese and tomato sandwiches

Not needing to impress anyone

Whipping up perfect eggnog

Photo printers

"Breathless" by The Corrs

Your old dorm

T-strap heels

Making gifts

Visiting your old high school

MTV edition cell phones

Bubblegum pink toenails on the beach

A reading journal

Listening to "Vacation" by the GoGo's

A marriage proposal

Ringlets

Fancier shopping bags stores use around the holidays

Abandoning guilt

Giving your mother's recipe your own spin

Acing an interview

Knowing how to set a table

Vinyl CD-Rs that look like 45s

Peach blush and lipstick

DVD camcorders

Decorative purse compacts

Pencil skirts

Hibernating for a weekend

Small changes yielding big results

Channeling your inner diva

Staying for the meeting at Weight Watchers

Gap Body

Clothing in neutral earth tones

Looking forward to something

George Foreman's
Lean Mean Fat Reducing Machine

Snapping out of a bad mood

Personal space

Getting caught under the mistletoe

Shopping for furniture

Mother's Day and Father's Day cards
that make your parents teary-eyed

Loading up on veggies

Knowing you don't have to be thin to be beautiful

Spa packages for girlfriends only

Echinacea

Ann Taylor Loft

Always knowing the top survey answers
when watching old *Family Feud* episodes

Showing tact

You're a perceptive Virgo chick

Your birth flower is the Jonquil (March)

Browsing at Crabtree and Evelyn

Free Super Saver Shipping on Amazon.com

Beer goggles

Never falling for the crash diet of the month

Wearing a tiara on your birthday

The fan letters you wrote as a preteen

A romantic New Year's Eve at home

Organic shampoo

Kickboxing workouts

Ballet slippers

Skipping the appetizer

Pachelbel's *Canon*

Your brokerage account

Watching the Miss America pageant

Shoe-shaped pushpins

The skeletons in your closet

A memory key

T-shirt bras

Adopt a Shelter Dog Month (October)

College all-nighters

Pepperidge Farm Mini Milanos

A simple "thank you" when someone compliments you

A ludicrous story in a tabloid

Pop-up blocking software

Driving by the house you grew up in

Your poker face

Shopping for vacation clothes

French fries with mozzarella and gravy

Believing in miracles

Your 401K plan

5-star accommodations

Your first game of Spin the Bottle

Regular periods

Ignoring the "what if's"

The Honda Civic del Sol

MAC makeup

Ballet-inspired fitness classes

Being multilingual

Saving sentimental greeting cards

Redbook magazine

Crashing a party

Outdoor fireplaces

Your obsessive-compulsiveness

A morning at the salon

Lycra

Your birthstone is topaz

Valentine messages in your local newspaper

Attending a World Series game

Punk chic

Lowlights

Nikki and Victor

Baileys on the rocks

Pumpkin face masks

Your state has no sales tax on clothes

b. Kliban cats

Mouthing off on epinions.com

New York accents

A long weekend in Acapulco

Negotiating a good deal

Getting something unpleasant out of the way

Buckle tops

Your wild friend who never judges

The man of your dreams purring in your ear

Holding off on salt to kick PMS

Your fierce cross-training routine

Finishing a book in one day

Reading the personals just for fun

Wood bangle bracelets

A weekend to-do list

Custom-built computers

Taking a class at NYU

He calls when he says he will

You love to mingle

The movie *9 to 5*

A yellow smiley face

Eyebrow threading

You're a fun-loving Aries chick

Upscale shopping plazas

Never forgetting to have fun

Imagining what you'd do if you hit the lottery

A personalized, steamy romance novel with you as the protagonist

An angel on your shoulder

Playing cards all night

The city skyline

Your comfy couch

Yankees Edition Monopoly

Your Saturday routine

Getting rid of your old perm

Friends you've had forever

Entenmann's chocolate chip cookies

Sleeping naked

The Nike Swoosh

The butterflies-in-your-stomach feeling

Lite beer

Clear bra straps

8-hour lip color

Traveling by train

Vanilla rum and Coke

Using a friend's employee discount
at a fabulous store

Finding the love of your life

The moment
when you finally "get" something

Loving drama

Elizabeth Taylor
(Charlotte's dog on *Sex and the City*)

Emerald-cut diamonds

The loathe of your life is moving out of state

Anti-virus software

The way you loathed Jerri on *Survivor*

Picking out your fine china pattern

A mai tai in a hollowed-out coconut

Socks that barely peek above your sneakers

The smell of spring

An ongoing flirtation

Late-night pizza delivery

Planning ahead

The Mall of America

Hatboxes

Making a snowman with your boyfriend

Peanuts cartoon strips

Crystal toe rings

Guys in oxford shirts and chinos

Color therapy

The Necklace by Guy deMaupassant

Overalls

Knowing just the right things to say

Practicing your serve

Hanger sachets

Champagne on Saturday

Chanel perfume

Lunges

Vodka and Pom

Party favors from Goodfortunes.com

Being able to roller skate backwards

Resistance band workouts

A Lands' End Overstocks catalog

Season premieres

The cosmetics counter at Saks

Origins Body Soufflé

Smooth skin

Movielink

Maribou high-heeled slippers

The Swarovski Crystal Heart Tic Tac Toe Set

Hosting your best friend's baby shower

Plans you didn't want to keep that were cancelled

Starbucks coffee

Trying on clothes you'd never wear in public

Budget Living magazine

The Style Network

Playing a game of Operation

A piece of clothing intended for teens that you buy anyway

24-hour room service in your hotel

Slouchy boots

No one but you knows your earrings are CZ

Confessions of a Shopaholic by Sophie Kinsella

Laugh-out-loud moments

Waking up on the right side of the bed

Making an audition tape for *Survivor*

Eating the pieces of fruit in sangria

Eye contact with a hunk

Break and bake cookies

The foods you hated as a kid and love now

Wearing one color head to toe

Fredericks of Hollywood's Boudoir Cafe

White gold

Lifetime TV's *Head 2 Toe*

Peppermint foot scrub

Wearing pink when you want to feel feminine

A lucky charm that always seems to work

Supersizing, once in a while

Aromatherapy in the kitchen

Seeing *Moving Out* on Broadway

Lariat necklaces

The Worst Case Scenario handbooks

Fe-mail Creations catalogs

You're a self-confident Capricorn chick

Coloring books for grown-ups

Cute luggage tags

A pink trench coat

Your stash of all-purpose emergency gifts

Big night glam fashion

Good luck

Rebecca by Daphne du Maurier

Your favorite celeb hosting *Saturday Night Live*

The Mazda Miata convertible

Flaunting your new pedicure

A dirt-cheap bargain

La Coste fitted tees

Foreign editions of your favorite magazine

Your old *Little House* books

7/18/99, the day David Cone
pitched a perfect game at Yankee Stadium

Airbrush makeup

AOL desktop themes

White Castle cheeseburgers

Waking up next to someone you love

Radiant-cut diamonds

Buying yourself a fabulous diamond cocktail ring

Airbrush pantyhose

Hair styling wax

A birth control pill for *men*

The Young and the Restless

Lucky magazine

Somebody having a crush on you

Patent leather clogs

Clothes that cling in the right places

Moving day

Coffee with cream

Buying a whole CD for one single song

Homemade baklava

The snooze button

Going to the Stanley Cup playoffs

Slingbacks

Cookie dough

Hummus and pita bread

Hippie chic

A cabin by the lake

The breast cancer pink ribbon temporary tattoo

Indie films

Emeril Live

Gourmet pizzas

Going to a football game of your alma mater

Finishing your thesis

Bold highlights

Free Internet access

Designer collars for your dog

A smooth day at the office

Mrs. Prindable's apples

Watching the Super Bowl halftime show in person

A bucket of golf balls at the driving range

Staying out all night

Being in the right place at the right time

Kicking ass at Wheel of Fortune

Fitness success stories

A Christmas wreath on the grill of your Jeep

Going for a tarot card reading

Custom handbags

SELF magazine

Watching *Dirty Dancing*

Your most treasured memory

The Food Network

Wearing violet when you want to make a change

Someone you truly admire

Making a spur of the moment decision

Your cleaning lady

A keyhole blouse

The first time in a relationship
that you're referred to as "girlfriend"

Omelettes on Sunday afternoon

Black and white photography

A boyfriend who adores you

Last-minute plans

Watercress and fruit salad

No money down car leases

Tiramisu

Wearing blue to exude an air of authority

End-of-the-year clearance

Oil-free makeup

London broil on garlic bread

Kisses on the cheek

Court TV's *Forensic Files*

Having a secret admirer

The first time you got drunk

A good practical joke

Swimming with dolphins in Cozumel

Because hindsight is often 20-20

Luxury SUVs

Chandelier earrings

Your train is 30 seconds later than you

You are an intelligent Gemini chick

Red wine is heart friendly

Business miles
in your personal frequent flyer account

Being bumped to first class

The sassy green M & M

The tattoo you decided not to get

Gross-out moments on *Fear Factor*

Economic SUV's

A huge salad for dinner

Buying everything in cash

Taking your own advice

The Book-of-the-Month selection
from your book club

Wearing cufflinks

Nail polish for your dog

A credit card size eye shadow palette

Crème Savers

Answering to no one but yourself

The Audi Quattro TT

Making your own beaded jewelry

Johnson and Johnson's Baby Oil

Joining the reader panel
of your favorite magazine

Playful makeup

Big dreams

California burgers

Survivor contestants you love to hate

Carvel ice cream cakes

Planning a theme party

Getting your big break

The wretched boss you no longer work for

Naughty piñatas at a bachelorette party

Knowing you took your vitamins today

The fashion staples you couldn't live without

Making a tray of tequila ice cubes and dropping one or two into your lemonade

Snuggling up by a warm fire

Your most official signature

Shakespeare bookends on your bookshelf

Your studio apartment

Glass roses

No errors of any kind on your resume

Mallwalking

Working out with a partner

The detours life often takes

The college grad rebates when you buy a car

Stick-on bras

Staying late and getting a lot of work done

Your undergrad *Intro to Psychology* class

Tree-trimming parties

Serving on a jury

The beaches of Southwest Florida

Sleeping off a vicious hangover

An internship

A piece of art you connect with

The groundhog seeing his shadow

Going to the symphony at Carnegie Hall

American League baseball teams

Cell phone insurance

Reading a censored book

Perky breasts

Love spells

Throwing an anti-Valentine's Day chocolate party

Quiet in the middle of the night

Sinking your toes into the warm sand

The word of the day

Old-school music

Sarcasm

A coupon for your birthday from your favorite store

Waking up an hour early

All of your crap that collects in your big purse

Your business card collection
from sixth grade

A funky artisan shop

Mini lint removers

Good directions

Breath strips

Reigning as the queen of your castle

Vogue magazine

A new pair of sunglasses

Antibacterial towelettes

Live journals

You're an optimistic Sagittarius chick

It's payday!

Online wish lists

Soup du jour

Personalized TV listings

Three cherries on your slot machine

Easter colors

Summer displays in stores

Candies shoes

for Chicks

Your favorite room in the house

Getting your entire security deposit back

Nordstrom

You can still do a cartwheel

Watching *Never Been Kissed*

Wearing something shockingly out of character

A helium balloon bouquet

Teaching an exercise class

Taking a class at the local adult school

Your boss actually values your opinions

A philosophical discussion

A champagne flute bouquet

President's Day sales

Biker chic

A horseshoe necklace

Bumper cars

Ghiradelli chocolates

Betsey Johnson's quirky designs

You don't bite your nails anymore

Snagging a job as a mystery shopper

Because you're not gullible

A mini sewing machine

The scent of Paul Mitchell hair products

A postcard from overseas

Working alone in the darkroom

People who just take themselves too seriously

Giving someone who's had too much to drink a ride home

Being able to stitch up a hem

That get-rich-quick infomercial you fell for

Yogic breathing

A brand new sketchpad

Feng shui-ing your cubicle

Because ectomorphs are voluptuous

Because endomorphs are naturally slender

Because mesomorphs are muscular

The cute *For Dummies* guy

A new workout outfit for motivation

Taking a midnight drive

Giving your hair a rest from chemical treatments

Not feeling bad on a single Valentine's Day

An afternoon in an art gallery

Watching movie rentals all day long

Egyptian cotton towels

Putting a painful past behind you

Diet Coke with lime

Photo editing software

January white sales

Remembering to look at the space between the wine and the cork before buying a bottle

Pocket PCs

It's your birthday!

Schoolgirl chic

Software that does your taxes for you

Touching the Stanley Cup

Turning your apartment into a home

Menswear chic

Gucci's Belted Clutch Bag

Your carefree attitude

Eye cream

Reducing the size of your pores

Guacamole

The loads of vitamin A in ruby red grapefruit

Orange light bulbs for instant sunshine

Training for a marathon

Your birth flower is the Sweet Pea (April)

Keeping clutter under control

Anticurl hair relaxers

Dancing naked in the privacy of your own home

Breaking up your workouts

Detangler spray

A scalp massage

A chocolate lover's cookbook

Thalassotherapy

Olive oil and egg yolk on your hair for 15 minutes

Anti-residue shampoo

Being able to wing it very well

Splashes of highlights

You're a logical Libra chick

Mission style furniture

A visceral reaction to artwork

Knowing how to match wine with food

Healthy Skin Month (November)

Bittersweet chocolate truffles

Realizing that although
the grass may look green, it usually isn't

Your parents raised you to be optimistic

Surviving an embarrassing moment

Alcohol-free fragrances

Not taking things personally

Taking your new relationship slowly

Signing up with a professional matchmaker

Teaching yourself a new language

Suave's versions of designer hair care

Researching your family tree

Reusable canvas grocery bags

The smell of your freshly painted apartment

Passing the bar exam on your first try

Being the sane one in the family

E-books

Alabama slammer shooters

Giving up something for Lent and sticking to it

Weirdo food combinations
that only you appreciate

A long bright scarf

Going to a fashion show

Browsing the couture collection
at Neiman Marcus

Capris with high-heeled boots

Western-style belt buckles

Bohemian chic

High quality shoeboxes

Seeing Rod Stewart in concert

The harpy that works in the next cubicle is out on vacation

Using acupressure to relieve stress

Board shorts

Mandarin collars

Doing something you really enjoy, even if you're not great at it

Sex releases endorphins

A clever aphorism

A picnic lunch at a scenic lookout

Turquoise and brown together

Multi-strand necklaces

Your morning muffin and latte

Daily facial cloths

Your birthstone is diamond

The antioxidants in cocoa

Practicing proper posture

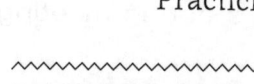

Sheer bronze shimmer powder

Trial sizes

A book that changes your life

Buying clothes after losing weight

Do-it-yourself brew kits

Reaching your 10 percent goal

Cutting the size tags out of your clothing

Bright green eye shadow

Brigitte Bardot-inspired hair

A big flower in your hair

Sporty chic

Stain sticks

Going for days without turning on your TV

Strange coincidences

Unexplained energy

An above-average annual review at work

Watching your favorite movie for the hundredth time

The Rabbit corkscrew

Keeping up with politics

Learning from your mistakes

Drawing stick figures during a boring meeting

Midriff-worthy abs

Swearing up and down
that you'll never drive a minivan

White jeans

Your favorite little black dress

Eyelid compresses

Being naturally outgoing

Filling your ice cube tray with fruit juice
to spruce up a glass of water

The *SELF* Magazine Challenge

Not taking the easy way out

An art house film night with the girls

Donating blood

Buying your cars
during the last week of the month

Post-summer department store sales

Automatic savings deductions
from your paycheck

Not judging yourself by your size

Drinking enough water

Glam chic

The health benefits
of moderate wine consumption

The scent of sunflowers

A Digital Sunrise clock

Weekend chic

Turing a bad hair day into
an "I don't care" day

Wearing your thong on the beach
in Rio de Janeiro

Riding on a gondola in Venice

An endless pot of coffee on a Sunday morning

Trying on couture fashions
you couldn't possibly afford

A cardboard sleeve
around your steaming coffee cup

Spending *hours* in one store

Going to a drive-in

No longer being a rookie in your field

A seafood dinner at Fisherman's Wharf
in San Francisco

Riding on the back of a Harley Davidson

Feminism

Pink pearls

Isaac Mizrahi at Target

Visiting your gyno annually

Having an attorney

Catching yourself
dwelling on something and stop

Direct deposit

Your Amazon.com Gold Box

Renter's insurance

Having three months' expenses
for emergencies

Your stock mutual funds

You're a confident Leo chick

Multimedia messaging

Picture caller ID

Free mobile-to-mobile minutes

Aerosoles

Makeup remover towelettes

A cashmere tunic

Lip stain

Make-your-own perfume kits

Trying the rock climbing wall at your gym

Going on safari

Knowing how to handle a rude question

A denim wrap dress

Shape magazine

Visiting a nude beach

Alphabetizing your library on a rainy weekend

Knowing how to deliver a punchline

Remembering how to conjugate French verbs

Name-dropping when appropriate

Asking for a raise and getting it

A denim skirt, tee shirt and flip-flops

Waiting room magazines you haven't read

Getting paid what you're worth

Making a great entrance

Kicking PMS

The theme song to *Survivor*

Marcasite jewelry

Holiday ankle socks

Cap sleeves

Escada Island Kiss

Donna Karan Cashmere Mist

Hot rollers

All of the flowers you receive for Administrative Professional's Day

Wet & Wild $1 cosmetics

A bamboo folding screen in your living room

Memories of playing *Twister*

Your one skirt that stays lint free

Matching your bras and panties

Doodling your name

Giving him an ultimatum

Ordering lunch at the office on Fridays

A mini heater under your desk in the winter

A ridiculously funny screwball comedy

www.diynetwork.com

Diamond initial pendants

Stashing a few extra dollars in your savings account

Getting out of a beauty rut

Your high school rival gained 20 pounds

Turquoise, sun yellow and hot pink

Taking your dog on a hike

Blogs

Fitness magazine

Your signature scent

Color-enhancing shampoo

A sweater shaver

Your favorite time of day

A spa vacation in Puerto Vallarta

Snowshoeing

Anti-wrinkle cream

Mixing your prints

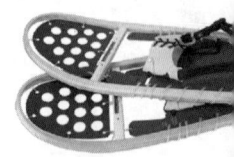

You used to love watching *Charles in Charge*

Your best friend never getting pissed if your call wakes her up

Hallmark Shoebox greetings

Sending a sexy e-mail

Designer handbag knockoffs

Your favorite store in the mall

Lunch at the mall's food court

Becky Bloomwood

A Kate Spade planner

A Lulu Guinness tote

Arden B

Sample sales

Bagel Day

Journey's *Greatest Hits*

You're a loyal Cancer chick

Caramel popcorn

A roomy leather satchel

Cutting out pictures of products you love

Lipstick with shimmer

Lots of pillows on your bed

Multi-tonal hair color

A yoga starter kit

A tennis bracelet

The smell of your favorite shampoo

Platform sandals

Depressing country songs

Hershey's Hugs

Dark chocolate and cabernet

Meeting a friend for lunch

Passing notes during a meeting

Drinks at a marina restaurant

Burning a cd of your favorite songs

Throwing a Final Four party

An afternoon at the planetarium

5-day nail color

Dillard's

A friend who shares her employee discount with you

Stiletto heels

Country stores

The perfect running shoe

Barneys Private Label

Neiman Marcus Last Call Clearance Centers

Grommeted leather belts

A cotton shirtdress in the springtime

Acting ladylike

Tortoiseshell eyeglass frames

Straightening irons

A new paddle brush

High cheekbones

Finding a discontinued product you love
at a closeout store

'60s chic

Jackie O sunglasses

A stainless steel espresso maker

A heated lash curler

Makeup palettes

Leather photo frames

Cheap shampoos
that work as well as expensive ones

Leap year

Keeping a diet diary

Eating peanut butter straight from the jar

A cool shower

Keeping your lipstick in the fridge

A friend who always plays devil's advocate

A long sweater coat

Eating something green at lunch and dinner

Finding your natural high

Being able to touch your toes

Hot milk with honey before bed

Rose petals in your bath

Being able to buy clothes that fit now,
not in five pounds

Super healing foods

Sweet potato chips

Maintaining your élan

Bare summer legs

A chignon

You own a real toolbox

Going on a money fast

Taking a dating break

Doing errands on your lunch hour

Having your split ends trimmed

Getting into law school

Open bar

Knowing how to hail a cab

Pictures of loved ones on your desk at work

Never having a thing to wear
even though your closet is full

Deciding to go back for your degree

The scent of hazelnut coffee

Something that happens accidentally on purpose

A bouquet of tulips

Hitting no red lights

Finishing a jigsaw puzzle

Reading anything by Shakespeare

How you loved *The Cat Ate My Gymsuit*

Going into seclusion for a weekend

Tending to see the good in people

Wanting to save the world

Looking back and having no regrets

Still being afraid of the dark

Overcoming a major fear

Listening to your old heavy metal CDs
from time to time

Feeling in control of your life

Spackling

You're an intense Scorpio chick

Being proud to be an American

Worn-in jeans

Nathan's French fries

V-necks

Watermelon Jolly Ranchers

Tae Bo

A clever advertisement

You made someone's day

Guys who smell good

Having your chart read by an astrologer

Knowing the difference between parfum,
eau de parfum, eau de toilette, and eau de cologne

Having your teddy bear
sit next to you on the couch

Misting champagne
on your damp hair for volume

Speaking to your plants

Because you recycle

Back-to-back episodes of *The Nanny*

Seeing the Eiffel Tower in person

Cosmopolitan's "Fun Fearless Females of the Year"

Clinique's 147 foundation shades

Ecco Bella chemical-free cosmetics

Being able to read between the lines

Lacey boy-cut panties

Working hard *and* playing hard

Smoky eyelids

Mac's lipstick shade B-Cup

Military chic

A friend's weight loss

Slant-tipped tweezers

Cutting out a cute cartoon

Ballet flats

Cargo miniskirts

Although you'll wonder about the road not taken, you're satisfied with the one you did

Reading your resume aloud before sending

American Eagle Outfitters

Glamour magazine's "Do's and Don'ts" column

A slim-fitting quilted coat

Designer rain boots

Buying a piece of clothing
in a color you never wear

The adorable puppies in
Estee Lauder's Pleasures ads

You understand mythical allusions
(Scylla and Charbidis)

Trying clothes on a virtual model

Thierry Mugler's Angel fragrance

Blush sticks

Adopt a Shelter Cat Month (June)

Green tea ice cubes to soothe irritated skin

A long thin scarf with jeans and a tee

Getting your feet in shape for sandal weather

Bright, wide stripes

Previewing books on Amazon.com

Buff Brides on Discovery's Health Channel

Having many of the characteristics
of your Zodiac sign

Ralph Lauren shampoo

Being comfortable with your body fat percentage

Cucumber keeps your hair shiny

Tea tree oil fights acne

Soy nourishes your nails and cuticles

Having at least one male friend

Choosing your own personal theme song

Colorful yoga mats

Sometimes thinking
you were truly born to shop

Recipe makeovers

Crocheted bikinis

Painting your tiny bathroom a bold, bright color

Sweater-lined jean jackets

Practicing your calligraphy

L'Occitane

Kitchen Aid appliances in trendy colors

Open-toe pedicure socks

Getting at least 1000 mg a day of calcium

Monogrammed perfume bottles

Berry lips for fair-skinned chicks

Orangey-red lips for medium-skinned chicks

Brick red lips for dark-skinned chicks

Eggnog in your bath for smooth skin

Jimmy Choo shoes

You're a strong-willed Aquarius chick

15 laughs a day for good health

A salad bowl and tripod set

100 calories less per day = 10 pounds less per year

Leather jewelry

He didn't call . . . and you're glad

A totally over-the-top outfit

Rhinestone candles

Travel and Leisure magazine

Cherry print

A fuzzy pair of mittens

Skinny belts

No VPL's . . . ever

Making a list of all your dreams

Swing skirts

Joy and Jake chenille pillows

Not letting your job title define you

Uptown chic

The money you paid for that LSAT prep course was totally worth it

Keeping a dream journal

A bath by candlelight

Waking up early to watch the sunrise

Buying yourself a birthday gift

Corny jokes

Red velvet cake on Valentine's Day

Riding on a swing set
for the first time in years

Afternoon tea at the Plaza hotel

A thermal wine chiller

Reservations at a hot restaurant

Going to a jazz club

Trying parasailing

Volunteering at a local high school's
Career Day

Going on a horseback riding vacation

Valerian in your tea relieves tension

Singles cruises

Cruises to nowhere

Buying holiday gifts for a family in need

Volunteering at a soup kitchen

Bidding at an auction

Going to a block party

Folding a fitted sheet with skill

A swank dinner soiree

Chick flicks

TV marathons on a holiday weekend

Elle Décor

Beat Generation writings

Trashy novels

Getting a motel room with your guy

Signing up for an e-mail reminder service

Trying a new ethnic food

Attending a murder mystery dinner

Throwing a '50s sock hop party

Almond-scented anything

Being outspoken

Your old Blondie cassettes

Referring to your closet as your "Wardrobe Department"

Madonna's *Like a Virgin* album

Listening to "Barracuda" by Heart after a searing breakup

Vermont maple syrup

Pigging out on Swedish Fish at the movies

Dirty Girl massage oil

Your grandparents' fiftieth anniversary party

Not answering a call you don't want to take
(thank you, caller ID)

Comfort food

Finding the perfect gift for someone

Because people always say you're hard to buy
for and you just don't see how!

Knowing jealousy is a waste of energy

Cooking a meal for your *entire* family

Winning a radio call-in contest

Sidewalk cafes

Your birth flower is the Lily of the Valley (May)

Giving someone a present for no reason at all

Buying a Tiffany & Co. rattle
for your brand new niece or nephew

Male/female jokes

Solving a wickedly hard brainteaser

Warm Krispy Kremes

VH1's *Behind the Music*

Checking your e-mail compulsively

Taking your 30th birthday in stride

Having just enough time
to make your connecting flight

Doing your cardio workout in your target zone

Living through your comp exams

Glamour gloves

An outfit that goes from day to night

Ankle boots

Distressed leather

Ultrasuede bedding

An A-line shift dress

Splurging at the dollar store

Elizabeth Arden's Spa in a Box

Big hair

You're a romantic Pisces chick

A fold-up treadmill in your closet

Taking your eBay business from part-time to full-time

Alternative Health magazine

Racer back sports bras

Flashy accessories with a simple outfit

Black panty liners under light underwear

Using up all of the hot water

Books with dust jackets

Water shoes

A colored oxford with a white collar and cuffs

Convertible bras

Diesel jeans

A night's worth of undisturbed sleep

Translucent powder

Cropped cardigans

Embroidered denim

Coordinating your five work outfits on Sunday night

Classical music to help you fall asleep

Ripping the advertisement cards out of a magazine before reading it

Keeping a bouquet on your bedside table

Splitting a sinful dessert

Scented glitter gel pens

Herbal eyelid compresses

Learning to snowboard

Eye shadow in purple shades

A gyno you click with

Spending a night in a haunted house

Having your girlfriends over for a chocolate tasting

Petroleum jelly to smooth your elbows

Consolidating your credit cards

E-mail updates from your favorite stores

Making yourself breakfast in bed

'60s inspired bold prints

A rosette pin on your hip

OP swimwear

Smart comedy

Batik tube tops

A silk wrap chemise

Blotting tissues

Coconut lime bubble bath

Kelly green capri pants in the springtime

Patent leather mules

Wendy's salads

Stability ball workouts

Crème brulee

Crate & Barrel

Dedicating a song on the radio

Burt's Bees moisturizer

Weekend room makeovers

Spoiling your dog rotten

Toast, juice, and fruit
to soothe your hangover

Reflexology socks

Being a sexy size 16

Chocolate covered Oreo-dipped strawberries

Frozen California Pizza Kitchen pizza
at the supermarket

A tiny tampon case to slip in your purse

A rhinestone belt buckle

Shag slippers

Nutella on waffles

Shimmering body powder

Taking a cab when you've had one too many

Seeing the Christmas Spectacular
at Radio City Music Hall

Trying bungee jumping

Reading magazines from back to front

Body fat monitor scales

Chocolate ganache

The Hermès Birkin Bag

The way your shoulder blades look
in a racer back tank

Your birthstone is sapphire

Knowing there are people in your life
you could ask for help if you needed it

Caswell-Massey almond soap
A brand new blank book
Your mantra
Extra innings when you've got fabulous seats
Old movies
A votive candle in a wine glass
Raiding the fridge at midnight
A designer who understands your body type
Going to a wedding on a yacht
A catalog of catalogs
Decorative wine stoppers
A surprise housewarming party (for you)
Invitation only sales
Your salary is double your age
Throwing a cookie exchange party
Going vegetarian
Wearing glasses solely as an accessory
Giving yourself a pep talk
Low-maintenance guys
Kahlua-flavored pina coladas
The soft music playing as you get a massage

Reading *Sassy* magazine as an adolescent

$5 palm readings at a carnival

Throwing a dessert and cordial party

Buying a Burberry collar for your dog

Instant shampoo spray

Secret Santa at work

Dancing on the bar

You're an understanding Taurus chick

Stripper exercise classes

Crescent rolls with herbed cheese

Anchovies on your pizza

Not smudging your pedicure

Eating linguine without looking like a slob

Nude fishnets

A white spaghetti strap tank top

Washout fuchsia streaks in your hair

Pink diamonds

Island music

Stewart's Root Beer

Psychedelic chic

Being able to fold a shirt
as neatly as they do at The Gap

Baring your legs

Debit cards

Low APRs

Promotional interest rates

Never having gone over your credit limit

Makeup with SPF

Memories of New Year's Eve 1999

Internet access in your hotel room

Flirting at an office party

Putting up a pink Christmas tree

YOU are your top priority

Emporio She

Hard Candy's nail polish shade "Trailer Trash"

A set of professional makeup brushes

www.ehow.com

Faded Glory clothes at Wal-Mart

Velour tracksuits

Do-it-yourself home improvements

Playing darts at a dive bar

Auntie Anne's pretzels

Muscle tee bikini tops

Heated seats in your car

Cabana pants

Miniscule lingerie in catalogs that looks like it wouldn't fit someone over 80 pounds

Friendship ESP

Duking the maitre'd for the top table

Knowing the 4 C's of choosing a diamond

A perfect bank shot

Half price date night at the movies

A hint of the catwalk in your everyday stride

You driver's license photo is so bad its good

New shoes that don't cause blisters

Hue hosiery

E-mail newsletters

Water resistant digital cameras

The way your mood lifts
during the spring and summer months

Your employer offers tuition reimbursement

Baby oil gel

Stopping for a few minutes
to watch a street performer

Trouser socks

X-rated lollipops at a bridal shower

A double shot of *espresso*

A hazelnut latte

Natural Health magazine

Chanel No. 19

A strand of holiday lights on your headboard

A round bed

Reserving a hot new novel at the library

Making a bed with perfect hospital corners

Your favorite magazine's website

Light-up closets

A sunken bathtub

A homemade mango hair mask

Sweetheart necklines

High neck tank tops

A slash neckline

Palazzo pants

Getting a royal flush
at video poker in Atlantic City

A.B.S. clothes

You're a spontaneous Sagittarius chick

Dolce & Gabbana

Juicy Couture

Getting a teaching job
in the district of your choice

Miu Miu

B-52 shooters

Barnes and Nobles with cafes

Drinks with cute names like "flirtini"

Blue and silver pens
to address your Hanukkah cards

A lime in your Diet Coke

Taking a guilt-free nap

Buying one formal place setting for yourself

Buying a bunch of greeting cards
to send whenever

Manolo Blahniks

Made-up words
that only you & your friends understand

Spending one month's rent
on two pairs of shoes

Saying what *everyone else* is thinking,
but is afraid to say

Denim bedding

Renting your boyfriend's dream car
for his birthday

A tube top and terry cloth short shorts

Being known as the crazy one among your friends

Argyle tights

Watches with diamond bezels

Coming attractions at the movies

Eating capers straight from the jar

Sunday crossword puzzles

Stargazing at a lookout point

Having a candlelight dinner for one

Avon mini lipstick samples

Barhopping

Sun-kissed cheeks

Pizzeria Uno's Pizza Skins

Renting a party bus

Evian skin care atomizer

Spray on Band-Aids

Paper towels with your favorite comic strips on them

Maxine from Hallmark

Gingham for spring

Shrimp in coconut sauce

Lipstick may protect your lips from lip cancer

A dry cleaner in your office complex

Slot machines in the Las Vegas airport

The infatuation stage of dating

A weekend on Cape Cod

Shopping at LL Bean's 24-hour store

Your 21st birthday

Going on a haunted hayride at Halloween

New Yorker magazine

Love potions

Onion dip made from soup mix

When a dating drought ends

Charmed reruns

Urban chic

Baby shampoo

The Victoria's Secret Million Dollar Bra and Panties

Designer workout clothes

Jose Cuervo

Seeing the Leaning Tower of Pisa in person

Converse Stadium Stars

Graduating from *Sassy* to *Jane*

All the celebs you'd like to make out with

White Barn candles

The "Rachel" hairstyle of the mid 1990s

Brow pencil

Great sex

Jones New York

In Style's "What's Hot Now" issue

Wearing your boyfriend's shirt

An extra umbrella in your car for emergencies

A dishwasher in your apartment

Cheese-filled pizza crust

Hanging up on your ex
when he calls you drunk at 2 A.M.

Spiked punch

Your mom sending you home with leftovers

Upscale stationery stores

A warming towel rack in the bathroom

Open-mic night

24-hour McDonald's

Two closets in your bedroom

Self-discovery notebooks

Trying to keep an open mind

Dooney and Bourke handbags

Wallpapering a wall
with ads for your favorite designers

People telling you
that you look like a celebrity

Nautical chic

Christian Dior's Logo Saddle Pouch

Chicken McNuggets

A silk parasol

Gerbera daisies

Stargazer lilies

A good cry

A romantic trattoria

Throwing a make-your-own pizza party

A Tiffany-style lamp in your living room

Lining your entire eye to make it look bigger

Foot Locker for Women

Getting ready for bathing suit season

Bikini waxes

Soft lips touching yours

Talbots

Your first love

You're a friendly Gemini chick

How Sally Brown always calls Linus
her "Sweet Baboo"

You never, ever betrayed a friend

Your birthstone is ruby

Never wearing the same outfit twice

Crying after the last episode of *Sex and the City*

Thinking of yourself as a femme fatale

Porn chic (in the bedroom at least . . .)

A horse and carriage ride
through Central Park

Socks with pom-poms

Stuffing your shoes with balled newspaper
to keep their shape

Star shaped Post-it notes

Copying down the lyrics to your favorite song

Playing *Outburst*

The Miracle Bra

Sending a Pajama Gram

Quiet neighbors

Sort of having a crush
on some 20-year old member of a boy band

Kevyn Aucoin's *Making Faces*

Mix and match bikinis

Saving all of your tax records

Layered tee shirts

J. Crew

Buying a box
of your favorite Girl Scout cookies

FCUK

Your jewelry collection

A PBA card in your wallet

Your Victoria's Secret Angel card

Film noir with a wicked femme fatale

Flavored teas

Packing for a long-awaited vacation

Button fly jeans

Having your taxes done well before April 15

Matchbook-sized disk drives

Annie Sez

Camouflage print capri pants

Heart-shaped soaps

A minimalist approach to home décor

A professional workshop day,
away from the office

Treating your parents to dinner

Bringing your new boyfriend home
for the holidays

Talking advice from *Debt Free by 30*

Not being a jealous and possessive girlfriend

Tying up all loose ends before you leave
the office to go on vacation

New exercise machines at the gym

Not breaking out before a big event

A screensaver on your cell phone

Body massage soap

A new pair of riding boots

Your favorite season of the year

Colored denim

Being home when Federal Express arrives

Toeless pantyhose

Frozen coffee drinks that taste like milkshakes

White gold and citrine

A wall of colors to choose from
at the nail salon

Salons that take walk-ins

A silk scarf as a belt

Someone you know calls into a radio show
while you're in the car listening

Girly chic

Deep fried onion rings

An intercom doorbell

Kitten heels

Hearing about the backup on the highway *before* you get on

Safari chic

Pale nails

All-in-one lather and shave razors

Domestic Violence Awareness Month (October)

Dove Promises

Getting yourself anywhere with the help of a map

An uncharacteristically warm winter day

Your period lasting only four days

Being under on the mileage on your lease

The person who is #1 on your speed dial

Self-healing

A bob with an imperfect side part

Colored mascara

75 percent off candy the week after Valentine's Day

Getting caught in the rain
when you have nowhere to be

Stocking up during a sale

Feasting on kiwi

White bean soup

The Louis Vuitton Dhanura Yoga Bag

Zagat guides

Choker necklaces

You wouldn't dare trim your own bangs

When someone says, "I love you" to you

Sunday brunch at a luxurious hotel

A Chanel tennis racket and balls

Double stick fashion tape

Remembering when MTV debuted

Having a little bit of Carrie, Samantha,
Charlotte and Miranda in you

Replicating a look you love from a magazine

Splashing in the pool like a child on a 90° day

Your favorite pair of panties

Photo coasters

Boycotting underwires

Chili pepper kitchen accessories

Clothes you can work and play in

Virtual makeover CDs

When someone tells you that your
weight loss/exercise regimen is an inspiration

Yoga sandals

White toothpaste on a zit

Playing dress up
and trying on all of your favorite outfits

Colored salt on your margarita glass

Laughing at the sheer ridiculousness
of the *Austin Powers* movies

The way your older brother
used to torture you in your teens

The *Arts and Leisure* section of the *NY Times*

Online resume posting

An inflatable bath pillow

The '80s Sasson Oo La La symbol

Houndstooth print

Your circa 1984 cut-off, off-the-shoulder
sweatshirt that says "Maniac"

Reading a book to a child that you read
when you were his or her age

Not analyzing *every* last detail
of your new relationship

Words like "gnarly" and "tubular"

You're a generous Leo chick

People with whom silence isn't awkward

Customer appreciation sales

Aveda Reviving Mist

Remembering to renew your license

Your best friend's boyfriend is perfect for her

You exfoliate regularly

Escaping from a bad date

Settling into a new job

In blackjack, you always hold at 17

Rimless sunglasses

Your best friend finally dumped her awful boyfriend

Looking good while you work out

Lash powder

Jacquard dishtowels

Crisp cotton

Not having to be thin to be sexy

Chain charm belts

Cocktail onions in your martini

Itty-bitty purses

A bold-print car coat

Making more time for yourself

A massaging bristle brush for your skin

Beaded silk accent pillows on your couch

Sleeveless turtlenecks

Setting up a paperback or magazine exchange at work

Culinary vacations

The first outfit you bring into the fitting room looks great

You don't fear the future

Woven paper baskets

99-cent hot oil treatments

Monogrammed towels

You graduated with honors

Sunless bronzing towelettes

Peppermint foot lotion

Purple, yellow, and green Mardi Gras beads

Getting your pedicure in a massage chair

Cute surfers

Having strong, unshakable opinions

The Today Sponge

Reflecting on how much you've accomplished
in the past year on New Year's Eve

Not allowing other people's priorities
to become your own

The contraceptive patch

Sending your parents on a tropical vacation
for their 30th anniversary

Hair glossing spray

Female condoms

Downloading an online Oscar ballot

A same-size sister to swap clothes with

Doing the electric slide at a wedding

Finally finding your prince
after too many frogs

Kissing and making up

Writing your own personal mission statement

The friend you've had since kindergarten

Learning to belly dance

An arm around your shoulder

One of your wishes comes true

The Cheesecake Factory

Running a fabric softener sheet over your hair
to eliminate static

Embroidered cocktail napkins

A big new card store in the neighborhood

An old mustang convertible

Lo mein

The Bell Jar by Sylvia Plath

Taking an eco-tourism vacation

Free samples at a gourmet food store

Being lost without your *TV Guide*

"No purchase necessary" contests

A sexy makeup session

A free handbag with your magazine subscription

Your favorite body part

New York and Company

Cyndi Lauper's *She's So Unusual*

A bit of healthy competition

Being a bit impulsive at times

Being ready to take on any curveball life throws you

Square appetizer trays

Inspiring chicks in the military

Your junior high obsession with New Kids on the Block

Faux crocodile accessories

Flipping the ends of your hair out

The small pleather $2 Jordache purses
you had in every color in the early '80s

Meeting with a nutritionist

You're an Aries chick
who loves storybook romances

Knowing how to use chopsticks

Managing to make yourself look human
even though you overslept

Barely-there makeup

Movie reviews in the paper

Likening yourself to a siren
from Greek mythology

Diamond ID jewelry

A friend has a spare set of your keys
in case you're looked out

A neighbor who'll keep an eye on your place
while you're away

The Jordache pony

OTC allergy meds

Licking the beaters after
you put the cake pans in the oven

Freezing your favorite candy bar before eating it

You and your friends
always make each other laugh

Free lunch

A mini clip-on reading light

Homemade ice cream

Restaurants with an outdoor patio

Slow dancing

Strobe lights

Black and white detective films

Holding a little baby

Finding the right hair dryer

Memories of your
childhood secret hiding place

Your old Barbie dolls in your parents' attic

Shakespearean insults

A thundering rainstorm in the Rainforest Café

A happy-go-lucky attitude

Never picking at a blemish

Getting into medical school

Vacationing in the mountains

Losing those last five pounds

Your birth flower is the rose (June)

A landlord
who promptly addresses any problems

Thinking about what you'd do
with an extra hour each day

Inventing your own signature cocktail

A new Tori Amos CD

Attending a film festival

A terrycloth turban on your head after a shower

Mod chic

On-the-dot punctuality

Getting your MBA

Ms. Magazine

Hitting the diner at 3 A.M. after a night out

The banana clips you wore
in your hair in high school

Cannoli-flavored gelato

Mailing out your holiday cards on time

Friendly salespeople

Taking an art class

Your unlisted phone number

Fresh-smelling hair

A piano player in your favorite restaurant
on Saturday night

Rum raisin ice cream

Salad *after* your main course

Never playing dumb

The jingle of your kitty's collar

The taste of a barbecued hamburger in July

Being frugal while your sister is a spendthrift

Passing the CPA exam

Spare ribs in a Chinese restaurant

Italian hot dogs

Shoulder pads in the '80s

Seeing a movie in the theater twice

Butterscotch blondies

Minimizer bras

How you loved the smell
of your dad's cologne as a child

Demi bras

A poinsettia in your apartment in December

The smell of hot pavement after a summer storm

The neon fad in the mid '80s

Leather Keds with rhinestones in the early '90s

Sweater weather

Pesto cream cheese

The soundtrack to your favorite TV show

No longer spending your weekdays
recovering from the weekend

Partying in Amsterdam

Getting rid of any pieces of clothing
that don't look absolutely fabulous on you

Getting into your pajamas at 6 P.M.

(Nearly) resolving your mother issues

Cult films

Knowing you can't change someone

Using movies as mood medication

Mohair pillows on your leather couch

A settee in your bedroom

Your bedroom looks like a boutique

Chocolate cherries

The marriage proposal
you weren't ready to say "yes" to

Stenciling a border around your bedroom wall

Down comforters

Putting a chocolate on your own pillow
on Saturday evenings

Photographs underneath the glass top
of your coffee table

A formal sit-down New Year's Eve dinner

The first day of summer

No overage charges

Italian red wines

Kettle chips

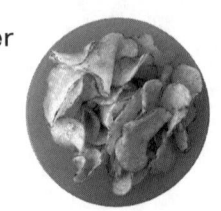

Your favorite player hitting a grand slam

Sensual music

Painless extraction of your wisdom tooth

People who can carry an intelligent conversation

Your birthday is on a holiday

Summer hours at work

Down vests

Your favorite piece of jewelry

Making an anonymous donation

Still making a wish
when you blow out the candles

An under-the-counter TV in your kitchen

Working through lunch to leave an hour early

Cocktail napkins as invitations for cocktail parties

Awkward pics of yourself from adolescence

Cheap shoes

Donning a wig for a different look

Heat patches for period pain

Keeping a wine journal

An announcement about you in your alumni newsletter

A juicy *E! True Hollywood Story*

Vitamin stores

Fettuccine Alfredo

Sexy plus-sized clothing

Receiving a cookie bouquet

Tie neck blouses

Matching your nail color to your sunglasses

Lane Bryant

The Avenue

It's your turn to choose what's for dinner

Getting the job based on your own merit, not because you have a connection

Health food stores

You're a charming Libra chick

A self-affirmation when you're feeling low

Framed degrees on your wall

Key ring notepads

Red licorice

Holiday postage stamps

A root beer float

National Professional Social Work Month (March)

Baked potatoes with chili and cheese

Designer notepads

Buying something only because it's on sale

Registering for your housewarming party

Having seniority in your department

Celebrity interviews

Back-to-back episodes
of your favorite TV show

A personalized horoscope

There is a day or week
honoring members of your profession

TV shows that annoy you,
but you watch them anyway

Joining a volleyball team
at the local adult school

Your 20-year high school reunion

Going to an alumni mixer

Your birthstone is turquoise

Bobby pins that match your hair color

Trivial Pursuit's Pop Culture edition

Lucite desk accessories

Scented drawer liners

Cinnamon toothpaste

Contrast stitching

A corsage pin

Chico's

Rolling Stone magazine

A white cotton dress

An all-purpose evening bag

A free makeup consultation

Entering a magazine writing contest

Your boyfriend proposes in *Glamour* magazine's "Man Message of the Month"

Making your cubicle more homey

A bowl of homemade chili

Decaf cappuccino

Mini Jansport bookbags

A celebrity clothing line

The haircut you didn't like is finally grown out

Birthstone jewelry

Going to see King Lear performed

Local restaurant delivery services

Craft fairs

A weekend spent antiquing

Free concerts in the park

Low-dose birth control pills

Tailgating before a football game

European accents

Samples at a cheese shop

A shoe sale at your favorite department store

Shopping during your favorite salesperson's shift

Joining Curves

Pictures of you in your high school uniform

Your nightmare online dating story

A gripping memoir

Your Slinky watch in the '80s

A spafinder.com gift certificate

Hands-free headsets

A cashmere sweater set

Having glamour shots taken

Nutritious fast food salads

Pina colada jellybeans at Easter time

The one food you cook/bake better than any you've ever had

E-cards

Boxes of chocolate with a "road map"

Car services

Specialty book clubs

Picking up a baton
and still knowing how to twirl it

Calling a talk radio hotline

Playing 20 Questions with friends

A friend who always gives perfect advice

Piano bars

Techno music

Calling somebody just to hear his or her voice

Extra cheese

Driving cross-country, coast to coast

Tricep extensions

Gourmet take-out meals

A list of books to read

A list of restaurants to try

Checking your bags

Reading at a sidewalk café

Professionally framing your diploma

A trip to Montreal

Decks of recipe cards

Getting paid to test cosmetic products

A Nicole Miller leash for your pup

You're a professional Capricorn chick

Chocolate Crème Oreos

Curbside baggage check at the airport

Extra packets of duck sauce

Toasting marshmallows over your stove

The last pair of jeans on the rack is your size

A backstage pass

A suspenseful thriller

Seaweed facial masks

Replicas of Princess phones

Cell phone pockets

Tanning towelettes

Spring training

Extra pickles

A veggie burger at the Hard Rock Café

Brownies with vanilla ice cream and hot fudge

Taking an origami class

Headphones to sample new albums
in a music megastore

Netflix

A fluffy powder puff

Carpenter jeans

House-sitting for a wealthy friend

Jambalaya

Brochures from your travel agent

The scent of your favorite shampoo

Heirloom jewelry

Pointy-toed shoes

Never forgetting a birthday or anniversary

Celebrity columnists in magazines

Ballroom dancing lessons

Poker night with the girls

Preferring the novel to the movie version

New Year's Eve at an upscale club

Trying a new special at a restaurant

A movie version that doesn't butcher the novel it's based upon

Toga parties

Being a style chameleon

Appliquéd jeans

Bring-a-single-friend parties

Satin baseball jackets

A glass of Riesling

Gucci Envy perfume

Undies that don't peek out of your pants

Gel blush

Evening primrose oil for PMS

Your stylist can fit you in at the last minute

An herbal body wrap

Cheese and crackers

Keeping your professional memberships current

A lei at a summer barbecue

Being invited to a luau

A hot cream manicure

Applying to business school

Always being up for a good time

Not feeling compelled
to forward chain e-mails

New fragrances

Making your own gift wrap

A tie-dyed dress

The perfect party outfit

Shell jewelry

You can uncork champagne
without risking an eye

A straw clutch

Blister Band-Aids

Clear Band-Aids

Lucite heels

Steve Maddens

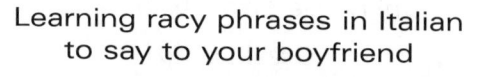

Learning racy phrases in Italian
to say to your boyfriend

Going to the beach in autumn

Allure magazine

Being on civil terms with a few exes

Leaving a bad party early

Not living vicariously through your relationships

Flipping through old scrapbooks

A heart rate watch to wear during your workouts

Only RSVPing "yes" when you really want to

Starting to fall for a guy
you initially wrote off as "not my type"

$5 clearance racks

Low-impact workouts to beat tension

Asking your teenage cousin's Magic 8-Ball
a question

Your one "Samantha Jones"-type friend

A terrycloth shower wrap

Cocktail glasses etched with your initial

An uncanny feeling that something good
is going to happen

Still celebrating Halloween

Online personality quizzes

Greek salad

Relaxing in a sauna

A mirror on the wall
to make the room look bigger

Trying on shoes

You're a Taurus chick
who is proud to be a label snob

Your birthstone is amethyst

Jogging on the beach

Window-shopping on Fifth Avenue

Potato skins with cheese, bacon bits,
and sour cream

Decadent appetizers

Browsing at the university bookstore

A feature you're frequently complimented on

A shortcut on the way home from work

Curling up with your favorite book

Horseradish cheese spread on garlic toast

Beverly Cleary's *Ramona Quimby* books
you read as a child

Your first trip abroad

The first weekend away
with your new boyfriend

The first time you refer to the guy you're dating
as your boyfriend

Raspberry iced tea

The anticipation of Friday
that you feel Thursday night

Black raspberry ice cream

Italian cooking shows

Cellulite cream

Cellulite wraps

Domino's Pizza

The shower music in *Psycho*

The perfect blow dry

A commercial that makes you
run out and buy a product

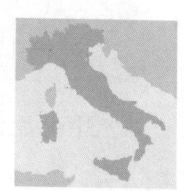

Wooden mules

A lace capelet

$20 off a $100 purchase

Velvet lined belts

Pop psychology books by Barbara DeAngelis

Shrimp cocktail in a chilled martini glass

Trying Indian food

Not needing a push-up bra

A good stretch before a workout

Birkenstock rain clogs

Monthly giveaways

Checking someone out without obviously staring

A bias-cut skirt

Message board friends

A Page-a-Day calendar version
of a book you love

Showing someone how to do something
you're very good at

A movie remake
of your favorite '70s TV show

Mom was right;
you did meet someone when you least expected it

Ankle bracelets

The end of a long day

Lipstick with SPF

A new briefcase

Aloe gel after shaving

The scent of your favorite men's cologne

Polka-dot cuffs on a striped shirt

Tab collars

Roll-sleeve shirts

Your ability to spot trends before they're trendy

Bucking the latest trends

In Style Home

Reading a book, cover to cover, in one day

Doing your own French twist

Taking a ride in a '70s hot rod

Wearing braids in your hair à la Dorothy

Nail polish shades with names like "Sin"

Gladiator sandals

A catalog from Nature's Jewelry

A rhinestone American flag belt buckle

Heart-shaped sunglasses
when you're feeling playful

Vintage chic

Vintage perfume

Duplicating a runway look
at a fraction of the cost

Decade parties

Using baby products on your adult skin

Hearty laughs you feel
all the way down in your belly

A bonus makeover issue
from your favorite magazine

A denim jacket with a sundress

Wearing sunblock all year long

Fragrance samplers

Virgin megastores

Sometimes Hallmark cards
make you teary-eyed

Salsa-of-the-month gift clubs

You're a sensuous Scorpio chick

A hair cuff around a low ponytail

Soup and a baguette from Au Bon Pain

Adding a few slices of cheese
to a jar of salsa and nuking it

Undereye concealer

Clean/Dirty laundry bags to bring on vacation

A do-it-yourself facial mask

Spoiling your dog
as badly as you would your baby

Having a good time almost anywhere

National Breast Cancer Awareness Month
(October)

Reggae music

Mini ice cream cakes

Not obsessing over your health,
but trying to be moderately healthful

Singing in the privacy of your car

Strawberry Cool Whip

Healthy recipe makeovers

Glass nail files

True crime TV movies

Jock Jams CDs

Listening to your old cassette tapes

Listening to your old 45s

Roof parties

Trying on opulent jewelry
you can't possibly afford

Sitting outside in the dark on a summer night

The first day of a weeklong vacation

Having a happy secret

Not having Sunday Dread
because you're off on Monday

Bar pies

The friends with whom you talk
about the same things but never get bored

A friend whom you don't have to be embarrassed
around when your stomach acts up

Free chips and salsa at Tex-Mex restaurants

Pictures of yourself from prior decades

Getting a card in the mail for no reason

College dorm memories

Heart jewelry

Taking a solitaire break at work

Hip-hop workouts

Hot towels on an airplane

Pictures of yourself that are so horrible
you know there's no way
you possibly look like that!

Salsa music

Ready-made margaritas

Hiking spas

Spiced coffee

A split of sparkling wine

Date night

Your first computer was a Commodore

Bass outlets

Liking the fact that you're so predictable

Amaretto coffee

Paper-thin Swiss cheese slices

Going to a Portuguese restaurant

Mood lighting

A hilarious drunken phone message from your best friend

Keeping a packed gym bag in the trunk

A bonfire on the beach

Port wine cheese

Eyebrow styling gel

Loofah sponges

Making French toast stuffed with cream cheese

Winning your first case

Romantic comedies

A wet-dry styling iron

Memories of the semester you studied abroad

Teeny espresso mugs

Accompanying your best friend
on a business trip

The first R-rated movie you snuck into

Hollywood's latest 20-something boytoy

Hollywood gossip

Soy milk in your coffee

Face cleansing wipes

Landing the hot new account
you'd been wishing for

A sweater vest over an oxford shirt

A great shampoo at the hair salon

Skincare products with shea butter

www.blissworld.com

Cashmere slippers

Not having to be thin to be happy

Never stiffing someone who deserves a tip

Computerized fitness trackers

Drinking your orange juice
out of a champagne flute

Enrolling in a personal enrichment course

Moving up and over on the salary guide

Online grad courses

Getting all of your ironing done on Sunday night

Book reviews in the Sunday paper

Macaroni and cheese from the box

Tangerine and hot pink

Three's Company reruns

Soup in a bread bowl

Sleep shorts

Going to a gay bar

5.0 megapixels

Velcro rollers

Tattoo-covering makeup

Buying a *Playgirl* for your best friend's bachelorette party

Touring a winery

Your team makes a comeback in the bottom of the ninth

You're a kind-hearted Cancer chick

A date you didn't have high hopes for surprises you

The relief of meeting a deadline at work

Knowing you didn't grow up as quickly as girls today do

A mimosa with breakfast

Seeing Madonna in concert

Upgrading your season ticket plan

The computer tech at work who can fix any problem

Rereading your teenage diaries

Going to an old-fashioned country fair

Daiquiris

Super Bowl commercials

Outdoor exercise classes

Making two leftover candy canes into a heart for Valentine's Day

Orange juice topped off with cranberry juice in an icy wine glass

Splurging on the hardcover edition of a book you're dying to read

Sleeping in your own bed after many nights away

Anything scampi

Your favorite department store being open until 11 P.M. the week before Christmas

Brick oven pizza

Making old jeans into cut-offs

A sparkly brooch

Cooking a new food

Naughty dice

Having your car detailed

The first day at a new job

5x magnification mirrors

Finishing your holiday shopping
well ahead of time

Always finding a reason to celebrate

Shots with X-rated names

Magnetic poetry kits

Celebrating your half birthday

Cajun salmon

Dwelling on a happy memory

Air-drying your hair

Your birth flower is the Larkspur (July)

Going for a trail ride

Trying an exotic food

All of the blank journals you intend to fill

Throwing a Christmas-in-June party

Red and green pens
to address your Christmas cards

Made-to-order fragrances

A washer and dryer in your condo unit

Passing the real estate licensing exam

Moving to a new city

A job transfer to an exciting city

Cold Case Files on A&E

Your boss is out sick

Going "shopping" in the office supply room

Running to the mall on your lunch hour

Comp time

The times in college when you had the munchies

Sick time that accrues

Time and a half

That clean, right out of the shower feeling

A health club in your office complex

A day at the office with few interruptions

Not skipping your weigh in
after a less than perfect week

At family gatherings, no one asking you nosy questions about your love life (or lack thereof)

A DND button on your office phone

Getting on the national "Do Not Call" list

Low APRs

Paying off your purchase
in the interest free period

Pastel colored light bulbs

A bulletin board of inspirational quotes

Buying a helium balloon for your birthday

Writing a letter to someone famous

Wearing something you usually don't
(a hat, a boa)

When a little child smiles at you or waves

Huge coffee mugs

Applying to be on a reality TV show

Checking out a local, lesser-known museum

Allowing yourself to be fixed up

White water rafting with friends

Linen spray

Hot air balloon rides

Being a literacy volunteer in your spare time

Flare jeans

A hairdresser who can replicate any style

Painless hair removal

Making $20 last in the nickel slots

White swimsuits that aren't see through

Personalized place cookies
at your dinner party

Lightweight running shoes

The 52 Deck series

Knowing how to jumpstart your car

Panty of the month clubs

Not allowing yourself to be taken advantage of

Anti-aging skin treatments

Reading a current issue of your college newspaper

Ankle-length jeans

Strategic placement of mistletoe

Eating lunch barefoot at a beachside café

Visiting an art gallery

Refusing a temp assignment
you just don't want

Breakfast for dinner

The precise moment you realize you're in love

Riding a double-decker bus in London

You're a trendy Aquarius chick

Flamenco gowns

A spring fling

A cool shot button on your hair dryer

Non-acetone nail polish remover

Seeing a bride and groom
being photographed in the park

Buying a trendy tee
to support cancer research

The second holes in your ears

Dramatic, smoky eyes

Having a different fragrance for each season

The smell in your apartment after baking

National Depression Education
and Awareness Month (October)

A classic board game as a hostess gift

Coral and turquoise

Makeup brush cleanser

A massaging bath pillow

A massaging backrest

Your steadfast belief
that people are inherently good

Balloon wine glasses

Oohing and aahing over puppies at the pet store

Your beautiful window boxes

Housebreaking your new puppy
isn't as horrendous as you imagined

Buying a few shares of stock
in a company you love

A trip to the movies with no loud teens
or ringing cell phones

Pear slivers and candied walnuts
on your salad

Making a drastic hairstyle change

Doing some freelance work on the side

Racer back tanks

A Dooney & Bourke faux crocodile bag

Men who aren't intimidated by successful women

Keeping a stash of coloring books and crayons
for when the mood strikes

Smirnoff Ice

Cosmopolitan's "Guy Search"

Surf shorts

Dr. Scholl's sandals

Cheap bikini separates

Shine serum

Hot stone massage

Renting a Jet Ski for an hour

Taking skiing lessons

Glossy covers on magazines

No nicks while shaving

Dessert at a patisserie

Cutting soda out of your diet

Coupons for birth control pills

Going on a ghost hunt

No tax on clothing

Duty free shopping

Throwing a Leap Year party

White denim

Your SAT score

A confident smile
because you know you look great

An even tan

Dumping an acquaintance who's a real downer

Doing something you're good at

Friends you can be 100 percent honest with

Having your best friend tag along
while you do errands

Making a "(Don't Want) To Do List"

Sticking to a somewhat regular
sleep schedule

Corrective concealer

Pizza with sausage and onions

A salesperson who will call you when a certain item goes on sale

Clairol.com's *Try It on Studio*

The older you get, the less you care what others think

Eyebrow shaping tools

Go-go boots

Virgin drinks

Powder brow fillers

Joining a club

Knowing the European equivalent of your size

Exercising in the park

Trying different meditation methods

New pillows for your bed

Hiking a challenging trail

Writing a love note to your mate

Finding out who your secret admirer is

Meeting with a life coach

Color treating shampoo

You're one of those lucky people who can eat anything and stay trim

Making an "I Did" list

Lesser-known artists performing at local clubs

Old pictures of your parents in hippie clothes

A store where you always find what you're looking for

Granny underwear when you feel bloated and gross

Getting picked for a magazine makeover

Buttonless, collarless jackets

Drop earrings

Great cheekbones (even if you have to fake them)

Homemade skin masks

Metallic fibers

Grecian chic

Wearing orange, red, and pink if you're a redhead

Visiting a botanical garden

Pairing a peasant top with capri pants

Yoga bags

Moccasins with a cotton mini dress

Elbow-length short sleeves

Self-tanning foam

You're a versatile Pisces chick

Riding the tram car on the boardwalk

Salt-water taffy on the boardwalk

Funky swizzle sticks

Two-piece martini glasses
that keep your drink icy cold

Linen bedding

A chandelier in your bedroom

Buying leather gloves while you're in Italy

Giving Tiffany and Co. gifts at weddings

Packing a wicker basket
and taking a romantic picnic

Vintage textiles

How wonderful it feels to come home
to a sparkling clean apartment

Watching Christmas cartoons
every year when they are broadcast

Wooden hair sticks

Unexpected great news

Floral-embellished flip-flops

Low-carb snacks

A girls' night out at the local bingo hall

Rhinestone hair claws

Not being able to get out of the hair salon without buying a ton of hair products

30-Minute Meals with Rachael Ray

Going to family reunion and catching up with long-lost relatives

Your sister isn't turning into Bridezilla during her wedding preparations

Money left over in your checking account at the end of the month

All-inclusive resorts

Sleeping under the stars

Liking at least ten different vegetables

Throwing an indoor barbeque in January

Your salad spinner

99-cent Hallmark cards

One-time yeast infection medication

High quality magazine pages

Getting your favorite cartoon characters on your checks

Spending one Christmas on an island or beach resort

Your mother's advice

Remembering how you used to play *Charlie's Angels* when you were a kid

Taking your look from everyday to extravagant

Untangling your most jumbled gold necklace

The PT Cruiser convertible

Purse-sized umbrellas

Salmon wontons

Weddings with cocktail hour food all night long

Stretch marks? Who cares!

Layering tank tops

Flavored half and half

Exotic fruit martinis

Tieback bandeau swimsuits

Letting go of unreal expectations

Sister Carrie by Theodore Dreiser

Golden lowlights for summer

A face-framing haircut

A baby tee that says "Bad Hair Day"

Tapas and wine

Rose quartz

White tequila

Wine-hued lips

Your pet's eccentricities

The feeling of microbeads on your skin

Thinking up names for your future children

Rereading your college essays

Your blazing red hair

A normal roommate

Those nasty layoff rumors proved to be untrue

Hair extensions

Tying your shirt at the waist
and showing your belly button

Letting the phone ring
when you don't feel like answering it

Lower-priced lines from hotsy-totsy designers

Free Scoop Day at Baskin Robbins

Being a member of a game show

Applying to be a contestant on *Jeopardy!*

Sun-bleached hair

Real Simple magazine

Going on a tour of a Hollywood studio

A catalog from The Paragon

Pom-poms trimming the cuffs of your pajamas

California Pizza Kitchen

Driving your new car off the lot

A hot pretzel from a street vendor in NYC

Wanda Sykes doing standup
on Comedy Central

Practicing your catwalk moves
in front of the mirror

24-hour roadside assistance

Wool sweaters that don't itch

Your all-purpose, go anywhere outfit

Hip length sweaters

Aeropostale

You've never colored your hair

If a new children's book by Judy Blume
came out, you'd buy it and read it

Handmade handbags

A squeeze on the elbow when you need it

Your A.M. coffee starts to brew
while you're still in bed

Enormous faux-gem rings

Pearlized leather

Ribbon belts

Oversized watches

Seeing kids wear the same black rubber
bracelets you wore in the '80s

A suede business card case

Registering on Classmates.com

You're a thrifty Virgo chick

High volume hair

Getting yourself out of credit card debt

Candles in the scents of yummy desserts

A romantic romp on the beach

Wearing fancy underwear everyday

Croco-embossed leather

A French purse

Giving your two weeks' notice
so you can move on to bigger and better things

Faux pearls

A leather clutch wallet

Keeping the inside of your car clean

Cell phone holders

Perfume roll-on

Summer colors like wisteria and azure

Getting a new cell phone

Keeping your distance after a break up

Getting in killer shape after a break up

A sidesplitting parody

A reconciliation with an ex
for the right reasons

Finding Mr. Right after years of dating tortures

Pink opal

Not living paycheck to paycheck

Clearing up a misunderstanding with a friend

Drinks on a rooftop bar

Going to a surprise thirtieth birthday party

Eyebrow stencils

Playing a game of beach volleyball

Knowing the difference
between fashionably late and fashionably rude

E-mail on your PDA

Boar bristle brushes

Ionic hairdryers

Epicurean shops

Keeping a list of all the books
you've ever read

A Tree Grows in Brooklyn by Betty Smith

Expensive chocolates

Your pre-adolescent obsession with the
Sweet Valley High series

Budget therapy with pop psychology books

Abba's *Greatest Hits*

A gossip session with a friend
about another friend you're on the outs with

A friend you can count on to be honest
when you go clothes shopping

A friend you can rationalize with
when eating large quantities of junk food

Snacking on fresh tomato slices
with salt in the summer

Pomegranate margaritas

Parting your hair on the other side

Throwing a (Long Island iced) tea party

Shaking up your workout routine

Wearing an oversized men's shirt

Remembering to send Mother's Day cards
to your friends with babies

Fuzzy slipper socks

Reading old journal entries

Visiting the haute couture shops in Paris

Having your dad's nose and your mom's smile

Trying a new international coffee

Reading in a hammock

A luscious daydream

A new cookbook

Watching the sun rise

Trying a new flavor of ice cream

Talking about your
most embarrassing moment with friends

Going to see a ballet

Blender drinks

Starting a savings account for your dream car

Foreign films with subtitles

Organizing your closet by color

People watching on a busy city street

Photo enhancing software

One-hour photo developing

Your favorite TV show on DVD

Vitabath

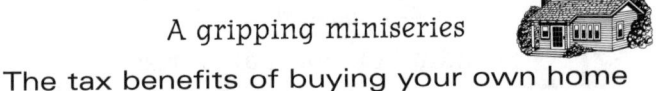

A gripping miniseries

The tax benefits of buying your own home

Pants with a built-in belt

A diamond and ruby heart necklace

Vacationing at a golf resort

Donating your hair to locksoflove.org

Online loop groups

Skipping the pantyhose

Listening to sexy music
while you get ready for a date

Putting a thin picture of yourself
on the refrigerator door

Feeling competent at your job

Knowing your parents raised you
to be a saver

Titillating Valentine's Day plans

A weekend at a bed and breakfast

Evening bags
shaped like Chinese takeout containers

A heart-to-heart conversation

Prevention of Animal Cruelty Month (April)

A spicy fragrance

Being pampered

A feeling of wanderlust

A panini maker

Wishbone necklaces

Online banking

Having both red and white wine glasses

A picnic backpack set

Two-tone gold

Wooden-handled straw purses

Luggage with wheels

Seamless undies

Week-long birthday celebrations

Gemini chicks + Libra men

Jelly flip-flops

Throwing a party for one

Being good about returning phone calls

A fitness evaluation at the gym

Rereading an Ogden Nash poem
you loved as a child

Your strong legs

Hopping on a plane to a warm destination
to beat the winter blahs

Voting

Liking your handwriting

Your best friend's ability
to rationalize anything at all

Stock shares in your company as a bonus

Fond memories of your first car

Donating your old clothes
to a battered women's shelter

Buffalo sauce

Bleu cheese

Spending the weekend at a friend's house

CD-Rs that look like your old 45s

The way your ring shines after you clean it

A photo computer mouse

Salsa dancing exercise classes

A spray of perfume on a cool light bulb

The smell of homemade cooking

An instrumental version of your favorite song

A coworker who brings you fresh fruit from her garden

Buy two, get one free bra sales

Always RSVPing promptly

Pulling up to a parking meter with leftover time on it

Playing Frisbee

Not smudging your new manicure on the way home

Maple cream chocolates

Always remembering where you parked your car

Raspberry cream chocolates

Trying a new restaurant based on a newspaper review

A realistic looking artificial houseplant
that you cannot kill

Sending yourself flowers at work

The cathartic feeling of throwing things away

Hosting a wine and cheese party

Making up a recipe of your own

Trying a new fragrance
every time you go to a department store

A new magazine

Fabric softener sheets to freshen your shoes

Throwing a Mardi Gras bash

Getting all dolled up on an ordinary day

Sleek kitchen gadgets

The smell of incense

Homemade wine

Throwing a taco party

Buying yourself a Christmas gift

Tennis sneakers

Walking in the sunshine on your lunch hour

Taking tango lessons

High quality, personalized stationery

Eating a pint of ice cream for dinner

Going to a genre of movie
you wouldn't ordinarily see

Sitting in the front row of a comedy club
and the comedian includes you in a joke

Trying on outrageous wigs

Your birthstone is pearl

Watches with interchangeable bezels

Watches with interchangeable straps

Illusion jewelry

Saving up your sick days for when you're well

Drive-up pharmacies

Snuggling up to a body pillow

A huge purse that holds absolutely everything

Having an espresso at the salon while you wait
for your treatment

The first time in spring that it's warm enough
to leave the windows open

Home decorating magazines

Dinner leftovers for lunch

Reading the want ads on Sunday,
just in case your dream job is waiting for you

The tingling in your legs after a brisk walk

Throwing chain letters in the garbage

Hot chocolate and popcorn

Sipping a mimosa at your desk
when everyone else thinks it's O.J.

Chenille sweaters

Slide necklaces

Fruit slices in chocolate fondue

Champagne punch

Catching reruns of '80s sitcoms
when you're home sick

Buying an ice cream from the Good Humor truck

Tailgating before a concert

Your cute mailman

Surviving a camping trip without a shower,
hair dryer, or cell phone

A rock-climbing wall at your gym

Low-fat salad dressing

Bladeless razors

Changing your mind
and not going into the office on Saturday

Planting a window box

A coworker you love to hate

The utter shamelessness of the office kiss-ass

Passing the Praxis with flying colors

Not forgetting to pack a toothbrush

Having the standardized test requirement
to your graduate program waived

Non-underwire bras

A day at the office
with no computer problems

Chicago

San Francisco

Concert tickets bought on eBay

Ultra-thin maxi pads

Yankee Candle's Midsummer's Night

The feeling you get walking into the office
on Friday morning

Mid-rise jeans

Grapefruit juice and vodka

Fabric covered boxes for storage

Farmer's markets

Sagittarius chicks + Gemini men

Oktoberfest parties

No cover charge for ladies

Free buffet during Happy Hour

Browsing in a toy store
as you pick out a gift for your niece

for Chicks

Pink sapphire

Hosiery shops

Armoire jewelry boxes

Ladies' Night at your favorite nightclub

Cocktail hour at weddings

Marquis-cut diamonds

Brand new furniture

Louis Vuitton's Damier line

Ben and Jerry's Cherry Garcia

Getting proofed

Playing skeeball on an amusement pier

Happy Birthday postage stamps

Mall gift certificates

White pencil to brighten your eyes

Manhattan at Christmastime

Your gym is extending its hours

Flutter sleeves

Photo handbags

Quesadilla makers

Microwaveable herbal neck wraps

Stupid prank calls you made as a kid before the advent of Caller ID

Ruched tees

Self-checkout counters at the supermarket

Hotel suites

Your birth flower is the gladiolus (August)

Express checkout

Hotel room minibars

No-smoking restaurants

Your desire to make yourself happy
is stronger than your desire
to please your parents

Browsing in airport shops

Can You Keep a Secret? by Sophie Kinsella

Queer Eye for the Straight Guy

Greek food

A bad habit you gave up

Calypso music

A high-heel shoe shaped cake server

Going to visit your old professor

An accent wall in your bedroom

The Breakfast Club

Elizabeth Arden's 5th Avenue perfume

Going through your old Teen Works binders

Taking the scenic route to work

Weight management multivitamins

Having a knack for retaining trivial information

A head-to-toe outfit for under $100

The feeling right before you fall asleep

Averting the gaze of someone
you don't want to talk to

Booking your plane fares after midnight

Paper lanterns

Canvas wine totes

Dipping anything in chocolate

Gel hair remover

Island chic

Tie-front bikini tops

Vaseline to keep hair dye
from staining your skin

University libraries

Yoga pants

American Business Women's Day (September 22)

A mini birthday cake for one

A big flower on your sandal

Washing your sheets in linen wash

A big breakfast to curb a hangover

The first time you cook dinner for your mate

The first time your mate cooks dinner for you

Mirabella magazine

The VW beetle

Commiserating with friends
after a rough day at work

Old songs that bring back vivid memories

Publishing your written work online

A pearl belt

No leaks in your toiletry case

Earth sign chicks aren't afraid to say no

Conking out on the couch
after a hard day at work

Having a little bit of Rachel, Monica,
and Phoebe in you

Codenames for atrocious coworkers

Orange toes for Halloween

A great soundtrack

Finding something decent to watch at 3 A.M.

Getting a free flight
in exchange for volunteering to be bumped

Watching *The Birdcage*

White sangria

A new episode of *Law and Order*

Flavored cream cheese

Bringing a bottle of wine to ceramics class

White pizza

Cheeseless pizza

Watching *Pretty in Pink*

Virtual flower bouquets

Estee Lauder's Beautiful

Colored jeans

How laid back people on the West Coast seem when you're from the East Coast

How high strung people on the East Coast seem when you're from the West Coast

White chocolate

Your accountant always gets your money back

Dunkin' Donuts with a drive through

The first time you got drunk

Heading up a committee at work

Making yourself an Easter basket

Muscle Fitness for Her magazine

Keytag membership cards

Godiva ice cream

Hand car washes

Movies in the park

Vertically striped pants

Redeeming your frequent flyer miles
for a ticket

Varying your exercise routine to avoid boredom

Energizing scents

Female celebs dating younger men

Your 25th birthday

Your 29th birthday

Tee shirts with your favorite team's logo
on them

A friend who lets you whine for a little while

Wedge heels

Ready-made Long Island Iced Teas

Hitting the mall at 7 A.M.
the day after Thanksgiving

Watching *Sixteen Candles*

Your unemployment claim is approved

Online mortgage calculators

Bibliotherapy
by Beverly West and Nancy Peske

Second careers

A $200 deductible

Someone says you look like you've lost weight when, in fact, you've gained a few

When a sex drought ends

Wildwood, NJ

The latest CD by No Doubt

Beers and BBQ

Drinking a sloe gin fizz

The shelves on your living room wall you installed perfectly

Seeing Aerosmith in concert

Halloween retail displays

Touring Europe

A framed four-leaf clover on your wall

Your old Poison cassettes

Santa Barbara, CA

Buying a discounted Rolex in Switzerland

Instead of staying up all night worrying about a problem, you decide to sleep on it

"Man! I Feel Like a Woman!" by Shania Twain

Having your mom come over to take care of you when you're sick

Treating your dog to some canine cuisine

Beans in your salad

Style on a shoestring

Winking at your date from across the room

Getting tucked in when you're sick

Fort Lauderdale, FL

Being complimented in front of people

Storing your perfume in the refrigerator during summer

Fat Free Cool Whip

Applying for a job you might not be qualified for, but you know you'd do a killer job at

You first brand new car

Aquarius chicks + Aquarius men

Shoe bags

Listening to your old Olivia Newton John albums

Hand washing your lingerie with baby shampoo

A French pedicure

Marie Claire magazine

Boston accents

You listen to your psychological, not biological, clock

Searching for recipes online

Watching *Grease*

Glamour's "How to Do Anything Better" guides

Getting promoted to manager

You don't suck in your stomach when naked in front of your mate

Colored contacts in aqua or amethyst

Your one friend who will go out to party no matter what, at a moment's notice

Your guy's smell on the pillow next to you

Being an extra in a movie

Your one friend who is never, ever in a crabby mood

Recognizing clothing from your favorite store on any body, anywhere

Getting over the fact that even though you're a size 8, your bridesmaid gown will be a 12

Bold, colorful accessories

Strawberry highlights

Having the summers off if you're a teacher

A friendship box

You're so over him

Clear liquors bring milder hangovers

Flapper chic

Not dating married men

Never smothering your mate

Expecting a lot from other people, but even more from yourself

Baby blond locks

Not waiting until you're engaged to pick out silver, fine china, and appliances to fill your kitchen

Censored *Sex and the City* reruns on TBS

The way supermodels and actresses look *sans* makeup

A spin-off of your favorite show

Deep conditioning your hair weekly

A layered, above-the-shoulder hair cut

Body contouring cream

A chocolate brown semi-permanent gloss hair color

Electric colors

Instant photo developing at the drug store

Online photo albums

Incredibly vivid dreams

A hot best man when you're the MOH

Pretzels dipped in ranch dressing

Feeling like a little girl on your birthday

E-mailing an author to rave about his or her book

Getting a reply!

Teaching a class at the local adult school

Organic Ben and Jerry's ice cream

Free upgraded shipping

Vintage furniture

White Russians

2 light coats of mascara

Salmon and buttercup yellow

Low-fuss men

Bragging about your tax refund

A boyfriend who keeps his mouth shut while you parallel park

Louis Vuitton hair cubes

A summer month with no weddings

Internet call waiting

Turn-down service at a ritzy hotel

The person in the fitting room before you didn't leave all of her rejects

Heart-shaped pretzels

A wine fridge in your kitchen

Squeezing half a lemon into your glass of water

Bargains you used to get at Stern's

Inflatable coolers

Baby wipes to get deodorant stains off clothing

A mini cooler the perfect size for a six-pack

The static sound when you play your old 45s

Not missing a patch when you shave your legs

Your checking account balances to the penny

Wal-Mart Supercenters

Oily skin doesn't age as quickly

A short wait at the DMV

Lime-flavored vodka

The latest Norah Jones CD

Jelly accessories

Country club chic

A cropped hooded sweat jacket over a bikini

Shirring on a bathing suit

A boyfriend who believes in more than thirty seconds of foreplay

Silk headbands

Realizing your parents were saints
for putting up with you during your teen years

Giving your pet only bottled water

Paying off your auto loan

Preferring to own rather than lease a car

Customized workouts

Colored condoms

Vegetarian hot dogs

Becoming more comfortable in your skin
with each passing year

You shampoo every other day

Fuzzy bath tablets

A cozy evening in front of the fireplace

Black and white advertisements

A handbag shaped like a corset

Low-carb ice cream

Taking a one-day crash course in something
you've always wanted to do

Cooking with herbs

Picking a bottle of wine
because of its neat-looking label

Stackable CD racks

Leo chicks + Aries men

Mosaic martini glasses

National Car Care Month (April)

Fruit-shaped candles

Purse-shaped chocolate candies

Body butter

A special issue from your favorite magazine

A wrap dress

Free refills

Spandex workout pants

The Breast Cancer Research Foundation

Reading in a coffee house

A "Last Supper" before you start your diet

Spinning shoes

Spa cuisine at home

Having body confidence

The Pillpak

Linen looks fine wrinkled

Quick-dry suntan lotion

Lipstick that stays on all day

Going polish-free in the summer

Coral lips in the summer

Chewable, minty-flavored birth control pills

Seeing a concert at Carnegie Hall

Caramelized onions in a recipe

Green apple-flavored vodka

Reading the comics

Renting a house on the Outer Banks

Wireless Internet capability

Never ordering just a salad on a date

The unconditional love
you share with someone

Online polls

Your birthstone is garnet

Baby tees that say "Bridesmaid"

Baby tees that say "Maid of Honor"

The apartment section of UrbanOutfitters.com

Flutter skirts

Call Block

A compliment on your perfume

Taking up golfing

Aged cheese

Watching the game at a sports bar

Memories of your date from hell

Going dateless

Having a trusty petsitter

Going home for the holidays

Mother-daughter shopping trips

A day trip to an outlet center

A feisty comeback to,
"Why are you still single?"

Hobby clubs

Wireless full-figure bras

Browsing in the cookbook aisle

A nighttime picnic

A trendy poncho

Wedding weekends

Sorbet hues for summer

Rainy day indoor picnics

Bagged salads

Perfect invitations for your party

People who RSVP on time

Having calling cards professionally printed

A loud cell phone talker who loses service

Your whites stay white

Shift dresses by Ann Taylor

Low-rent apartments

A mentor who inspires you

Video cameras that weigh less than a pound

More good love days
than your horoscope predicts

Year-round clothing

Iced coffee syrup

Setting up your own store on eBay

Suits for under $100

Earrings under five dollars

Tanning without burning

Being able to communicate with your pet

Hybrid cars

Electronic airline tickets

Blister band-aids

Making your own jewelry

Country chic

Perfumed soap in your lingerie drawer

New bath towels

Bringing your own tools to a pedicure

Cold wax hair removal

The two-second waiting period

between shots on your digital camera

Painting your toes in a jiff when
you decide to wear sandals at the last minute

Being chosen by your boss
to go to a trade show

Lifetime Original Movies

Appreciating that your parents
often told you "no"

Crystal Light

Kimono tunics

A cool, summer breeze on your bare shoulders

Not getting caught doing the Walk of Shame

BCBG

Bebe

The wildest of your friends
was the first to settle down

You got your boss's Fed Ex package
to the drop on time

Billboard magazine

An outfit that flatters you from any angle

The way your stylist blows at your hair

Cell phones mean you never have to put a
public phone's filthy receiver near your mouth

His palm on the small of your back

That weak-in-the-knees feeling

Body gloss

Stretch mark cream

The one bad habit
you have no intention of ever breaking

Creative networking

Surviving a layoff

Not regretting any major choices you made

Shorts that flatter you

Sleeping with a stuffed animal

Your quirky food rituals

A tomato red beach towel

De-wrinkle sprays

Fire sign chicks are always up for a challenge

Finding your car keys

A sunny forecast

An invitation that says "No Gifts"

Board games for adults

A kiss on your bare shoulder

Someone you only invited out of obligation
RSVPs "No"

You remember phone numbers

after dialing them only once

You don't know how you lived through 8 A.M. classes 3 times per week

Saving a gift certificate for a rainy day

All of the books in your favorite series

Your parallel parking skills

The new car smell

Natural therapies are covered by your insurance plan

Giving yourself a health makeover

Getting a part-time job at a university so you can take graduate courses for free

Mindfulness meditation

Transcendental meditation

Walking arm-in-arm

Chocolate roses on Valentine's Day

M & Ms in any color you choose

A sterling silver compact

Doing the YMCA dance

Men who put the toilet seat down

A Hawaiian print dress from Hawaii

Winning a prize at a carnival

Platinum jewelry

Pepper jack cheese

Black and white scrapbooking

You and your girlfriends all have pet names for each other

Your friend is dealing with her divorce very well

Freestyle cruising

Having your car painted a custom color

The Body Shop

Memorial Day weekend

Not being inundated with junk mail

Bath and Body Works

Fearing that you're overdressed, then finding out that you're not

Belated birthday cards

A bellyaching laugh

Taking dance lessons

Phone calls home while you're away on a business trip

Victoria magazine

Magazines about organic lifestyles

Discount stores

Buying your pregnant sister
a Kate Spade diaper bag

Bath massagers

Chip and dip servers

Confetti in greeting cards

You're the shutterbug out of all your friends

A hand massage

Getting your least favorite chore out of the way

Having a friend drop by your office

A 100 percent work-free weekend

Calling in sick and spoiling yourself all day
on February 29th

Old Grace Kelly movies

X-rated pasta shapes
for your sister's bachelorette party

Cheesecake for dinner

You believe in miracles

A 10-minute neck massage in the mall

Late dinners

Watching *Breakfast at Tiffany's*

Filling your Christmas stocking

Using a copy of a favorite photo as a bookmark

A weekend on a houseboat

Shopping for your first apartment

Inscribed jewelry

A toddler sitting on your lap

Your business card makes your job
sound much more important than it actually is

Drive-up ATMs

Relaxation exercises you can do
right at your desk to de-stress at work

Lining your pans before using
to avoid messy clean-ups

A travel agent who knows exactly what you want

Preferring to achieve happiness
and perfection

A two-piece "Best Friends" key chain

Flexible cell phone plans

A star you love joins your favorite TV show

Getting used books dirt cheap

Always being one step ahead

All of your friend's birthdays
are marked on your calendar

A floating chaise with a beverage holder

Late-night food runs

Keeping a grade school love note

Collecting matchbooks
from all the fancy restaurants you've been to

TV shows without stereotypical characters

Venice Beach

Cutting your hair one week before a big event

Going on a tour of Alcatraz

A bag of Reese's pieces

Doing a jigsaw puzzle while snowed in

A winter day trip to the beach

Eating Burger King on your best dishes

Double dates

Throwing an early Halloween party
on Friday, October 13th

Tossing coins into the Trevi fountain
and making a wish

A glass bottom boat ride

Birthday parties for your dog

Baking cookies for your friends

You can't believe that the store clerk
would call a hot babe like you "Ma'am"

Jewelry that shimmers wildly

Capricorn chicks + Taurus men

Getting the best seat in the house

Even if you didn't need the money, you like your job and might keep it (part-time at least)

Having the support of people around you during a tough time

Doing the wave at a hockey game

Saving old ticket stubs

Christmas Eve midnight mass with your best friend followed by a diner run

The Bon Voyage party your parents threw before you spend a semester abroad

Casino parties

Around the world parties

Running a half marathon

A rain shower that abates until you're inside

Sheer T-shirts

Foreigner's *Complete Greatest Hits*

The first time you wear a great outfit

Skirted bikini bottoms

A short, spiky hairdo

Treating yourself to a stack of new books, even if you have no time to read them

Remembering all your passwords

Three-step skincare systems

A professional closet makeover

Making a tray of vodka ice cubes
and dropping one or two
into your OJ or cranberry juice

Including fast food in your weight-loss plan

Thickening mascara

Lengthening mascara

A new look that takes a few years off

Grilled salmon and pinot noir

Being a free spirit

Your little black book

Blackhead extractors

R-rated fortune cookies

Teacher Appreciation Week (early May)

Stopping for a bottle of wine
on the way home from work

Half-price, discontinued makeup

Relishing the solitude of living alone

Fresh slices of watermelon in the summer

Shakespeare in the Park in New York City

Imagining what it would be like
to be filthy rich

Boardwalk food

Finding tons of uses
for everyday household supplies

Visiting your college campus years later

Boudoir pillows

All the episodes you spent
rooting for Carrie and Big

An instant rapport with your interviewer

Upgrading your car stereo system

A mesh beach tote

A patriotic bikini for the Fourth of July

A stack of catalogs to peruse

BYOB restaurants

Your birth flower is the Aster (September)

Your mate's special pet name for you

Laid-back summer dates

L.A.M.B. clothes and accessories

Practicing your Qi Gong religiously

Dressing well

A car that gets good gas mileage

Seasonal part-time work for extra cash

Getting your picture taken with Santa

Shoe addictions

Having your picture taken with a celebrity

Black-tie affairs

Cleaning out your desk at work

Any reason to buy a new outfit

Brie cheese and flatbread

Gingerbread cookies

Because you cried
during the last episode of *Friends*

Winning a free month at your gym

The new instructor of your exercise class
is better than the old one

Taking a boot camp class at the gym

Mileage reimbursement at work

Getting a company car

Finally getting your expense check

Redesigning your kitchen

Luxury townhouses

Your cozy studio

Your cash lasts until payday

Libra chicks + Gemini men

Making contacts in your graduate seminar

10 percent off
when you open a store charge account

Being your own interior designer

Taking a flower arranging class

Your checking account
has never been overdrawn

Being nice, even when it kills you

Being able do both MLA and APA citations

Giving your friends party favors
at your birthday dinner

Steaming hot showers

Margaret Simon

The crush you had in grade school
on your best friend's brother

Not having to stay out all night
for it to be a good one

Looking better now
than you did in high school

Doing things you really care about

Imagining what you'll look like
when you're pregnant one day

Throwing a spa party

Giving flip-flops as favors at your spa party

Effortless glamour

Curling mascara

Unisex cologne

ESP between you and a friend

Pink champagne

Buy One, Get One For a Penny sales

24-hour gyms

Seasoned fries

Heart-shaped measuring spoons

Getting your hands on a pair
of company box seat tickets

Bundling up to go to a football game

Department stores
that don't use flimsy plastic bags

Colored Post-it flags

The smell of burning incense

Catching some good gossip at the hair salon

Pulp-free OJ

Salesclerks at upscale boutiques without attitudes

Nail polish that lasts so long on your toes

Cooking dinner for your friends

Outdoor happy hours

Bergdorf Goodman

Making gift tags from old greeting cards

Neiman Marcus

Casinos on cruise ships

Going to a '70s style disco

Dancing on the stage in a club

30-hour work weeks

Roses sprayed black for Halloween

Drew Barrymore movies

Comfortable but unstylish clothing you wouldn't dare leave the house in

Breaking even on your trip to Vegas

Winning a celebrity look-alike contest

Getting a buzz from one glass of wine

Snapple Lemonade Iced Tea

Remakes of old classic songs

Ben and Jerry's Peace Pops

A Pier 1 Imports Clearance Store

Your professional portfolio

A summer snack of pineapple chunks and kiwi

Somehow knowing all of the words to songs you can't stand

Time when you just need to be alone

Catalogs with cheap junk
that are fun to browse through

Sitting at a lucky slot machine

Doing the Macarena at a wedding

Hot new bar accessories

A friend who's your exact opposite

Your mother drags you to a tricky tray
with her and you win something

Homemade pizza

Kiosks in the mall with handmade jewelry

Noticing the typo in your e-mail
before you hit "Send"

A new coworker you instantly hit it off with

Saketinis

Your early '80s celebrity crushes

Soothing aloe on your sunburn

The Unsend feature in your e-mail

Dealing with a clogged sink
without calling the plumber

Filling in your brows

Ruby jewelry

Amethyst jewelry

A trip to Aruba

Handbag parties

Looking through your yearbook

Not knowing what a virgin was in '84
when Madonna's song came out

Moo shu pork

Browsing at Chef Central

Walk-in closets

Master bathrooms

Dance remixes of '80s songs

Emerald jewelry

Bathing suits that don't ride up

The great feeling you get when your place
is sparkling clean

A cute delivery guy

Virgo chicks + Scorpio men

A coupon for your next purchase

Cooking without making a mess

Helping your little sister shop
for her dorm room

Factory seconds

Chinese style slippers

Saying something really mean, but
your best friend knows you aren't a mean person

The crazy places you did it

Sweating off some tension

Affordable luxury cars

Still being able to do a split

Harper's Bazaar magazine

Surfer chic

A friend whose parties are always fabulous

Clinique Happy

The first snow of the season

Your birthstone is aquamarine

Prime rib dinners

Not keeping track of who calls whom

A new buffer block

Friends who can see you
after you've been sick and haven't showered
in four days, and you don't feel funny

A friend whose refrigerator you can
open and take from without asking first

Your new boyfriend has a sailboat

Harmless pranks

Soothing a mosquito bite with a cold tea bag

Watching the
"Girls Just Want to Have Fun" video

Books about Barbie

Sniff tissues

Extra spending money for your vacation

Reminiscing over your Prom photos

No dishes in the sink

Looking back, you don't know how you ever made it through your inorganic chemistry classes

A mini paraffin bath

Neighbors who mind their own business

Mother-of-pearl jewelry

Snakeprint heels

Embroidered wet bathing suit bags

Drug store cologne you used to give your mother as a gift

Playing footsies

Reading a wide variety of literature

Free samples at the food court

Overhearing something nice being said about you

Ice in your juice to cut some calories

Popping bubble wrap on a stressful day

Reading for a few minutes before bed each night

Cherry-flavored Chapstick

Plush chairs at local bookstores

Treating yourself to a Cinnabon

The feel of cold perfume as it spritzes your skin

A new planner

Silver nail polish

Going to Oktoberfest in Germany

Not having to wait for a table in a restaurant

The awkward second before a first kiss

The excitement you feel while unwrapping a gift

Going without makeup

A good car mechanic

Baltic & Mediterranean in Monopoly, even though they're the cheapest

Yoga parties

Throwing a fancy luncheon

The gradations of your friendships

A satisfying crying jag, once in a while

Three-day emergency diets

Applying perfect makeup in a rearview mirror

The sad fulfillment of finishing an awesome book

The first day of a new semester

The red wine stain on your carpet came out

Avoiding a speeding ticket
with a little charm and a smile

Baccarat crystal

Pink Swiss army knives

Foot massagers

National Nutrition Month (March)

Books of poetry

Cancer chicks + Scorpio men

The *Anastasia Krupnik* books you loved as a child

More note cards than you could ever write

A catalog from Red Envelope

A friend who's never shocked,
no matter what you tell her

Agatha Christie mysteries

Browsing at the merchandise at Starbucks

Flashdance chic circa early '80s

One-hit wonders

Because you managed to survive
before the advent of cell phones

You snagged a pair of hard-to-get tickets

Lingerie tops with jeans

A rich friend with a tiki bar
in his or her backyard

Catching a foul ball at Yankee Stadium

Using a fake name with a creepy guy at a bar

Deleting voice-mails from an ex

Sharing a bubble bath

You're likely to see a female president
in your lifetime

A perfect white tank top and silk skirt

Drive-by spying

Pool parties

When someone goes out of his or her way for you

Sparkling seltzer in a wine glass
when you don't feel like drinking

Successfully tackling a do-it-yourself project

Stenciling on your walls

Writing a friend a letter instead of calling

Aloha prints on summer clothes

Flavored pretzel pieces

Facial masks with oatmeal

Heathered colors

Not being paranoid about safety,
but being careful

Getting dressed up just because you feel like it

The Lab puppies in Cottonelle ads

Having a backup can of shaving gel
in case you run out mid-shower

The best wedding you've ever attended

Boston Cream Pie

Rekindling a past relationship

Feeling superior when you spot a grammatical
error that the magazine's copy editor missed

Meeting a celebrity

Getting a house key from your boyfriend

Babysitting for a friend

Browsing at a flea market

Cheering up a friend who was stood up

Gumball ponytail holders

Cosmopolitan's online Pap test reminder

Shampoo and conditioner in one

Your birth control pills help beat acne

Sending a risqué postcard from the beach
to a friend who is left at home

Dipping your feet in a pool

Not having asked yourself
"What's wrong with me?" in a really long time

Forming a craft group

Corduroy jean jackets

Ordering a Happy Meal

Interior paints by your favorite designer

Laughing too loud

Your new top-of-the-line mountain bike

A new iSight camera

A gift certificate to your salon

Shield sunglasses

White chocolate mousse with summer berries

A home gym

A shopping spree at the art supply store

Lazy afternoons

Your stomach crunches paid off

Not telling your friends every detail

Limeade and beer in a pitcher with ice

Online photo prints for 22 cents

Canvas totes with leather trim

The first day of autumn

Citrus tooth paste

Knowing your dad will always spot you a few dollars when you're low on cash

Sending your mom a VT bear on Mother's Day

Having a healthy level of competitiveness

A pool in your gym

Nine and Co. clothing

Liz Claiborne

Lace eyelet in the summer

Having class

A cashmere twin set

Black, white, and gray crew neck t-shirts

Capris with heels

Keeping job stress to a minimum

Making a pre-vacation checklist

Afternoon dates

It's your turn to lead the discussion at your book club

Red sheets on your bed

A barbecue in the rain

Trying something outdoorsy that you've never done before

A late-night walk (not by yourself!)

A wedding in a gorgeous cathedral

Tying your boyfriend's tie for him

Driving by your old elementary school

Playing hooky from work with your
best friend and heading to a far away mall

The summer you spent working on the boardwalk

Girls who still play with dolls at 12

Distressed denim

Because water sign chicks
are protective of their friends

Using subject-verb agreement properly

Always buckling up

Winning a Halloween costume contest

The special bond you share with your sibling

Being a twin

Flip-flops for under $5

Free Iced Coffee Day at Dunkin' Donuts

Arriving at work five minutes early for once

Mailing yourself a greeting card

Morning news shows
while you're getting ready for work

Personalized Stacy Claire Boyd note cards

Your breasts are natural

A friend calls to check on you
when you're not feeling well

A handful of green M & Ms

Your favorite celeb on *Oprah*

Saving greeting cards over the years

Checking out your butt in the mirror

Catching a softball game
in a neighborhood park

Your sexiest shoes

Lingerie in your favorite color

Successfully conquering a mouse
in your apartment

Pineapple body scrub

Good in-flight movies

Adventure travel

First time buyer interest rates

Polka-dot laptop cases

The tension in the air at a
Yankees-Red Sox ballgame

Your collection of takeout menus

Marabou slippers

Painting your living room plum

Having friends over for cake and coffee

Feeling the cool water on your thighs
as you wade in the pool

Workout DVDs

Donating a few cans to a Thanksgiving food drive

A liquid lunch

Iridescent eye shadow

Chicken Caesar salad pizza

Weight Watchers magazine

Monogramming your Nikes

Morning workouts

Cold water to speed dry your nail polish

Got Milk? ads

Bragging once in a while

Backseam pantyhose

Visiting the pyramids in Egypt

Going on a solo vacation for a big birthday

Detangling with a wide tooth comb

A whole apartment all to yourself

Remembering to have your oil changed

Hand-making your own paper

Shopping at Bloomingdale's

Mall directories

Buying a Burberry bag at Harrod's in London

An officemate brings in donuts for everyone

Fajita makers

Friendship bracelets

Williams-Sonoma cookbooks

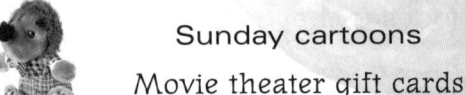

Sunday cartoons

Movie theater gift cards

Buying yourself a drugstore stuffed animal for Valentine's Day

"White Flag" by Dido

Hanging a Chanel shopping bag from your doorknob as a method of interior design

Looking studious in glasses

Penciling in a fake birthmark

Heart shaped cake pans

Talking to your fish

Your favorite performer will be in the area

Seeing Bon Jovi in concert

Being told you're smart

Being told you're sexy

The Volkswagen Cabrio

Hearing the words,
"We'd like to offer you the position."

Dressing to match your moods

Learning to tango

Buy three, get one free Hallmark cards

Going to a rally

Drinking a zombie at a tiki bar

Getting more than one invitation
and having to decide which to accept

Not sweating . . . glowing

A Sur La Table catalog

Your long distance relationship becomes local

The scent of a candle store

The scent of a coffee house

An open shirt over a turtleneck

Iced latte

Day-to-night handbags

A guy past 18 who's not into video games

Finding out the sex of your future godchild

Scrapping your cooking plans and ordering out

Adding an extra set to your workout

Someone you have a secret crush on asks you out

Deciding you no longer need
to see your therapist

A presentation you were nervous about making went well

Zigzag stem cocktail glasses

Personal days

Your neighbor with the barking dog is moving

Fendi bags

Making beautiful table centerpieces

Full health benefits

Leather cleaner for your handbag

Painting the town red

Gift certificates
where you choose the restaurant

Aries chicks + Libra men

A pool in your complex

A personalized workout program
on your treadmill

Being naturally muscular

A quality opening act at a concert

Closeout offers on the Internet

A former nerd who turned great looking
and successful at your high school reunion

Mexican coffee

Getting into the holiday spirit

Finding that you like someone
you thought you wouldn't

$2.50 per item dry cleaners

Keeping a travel journal

The Tower of Terror at Disney's MGM Studios

Big, strong hands overlapping yours

Weird NJ magazine

Previewing an exercise tape
while eating fast food

Stretch SUVs for a night on the town

An event you dreaded is over

A king-sized bed in your hotel room

Lindt truffles

Visiting the Statue of Liberty

Graduating from roommate to no roommate

A $10 copay

Making your last car payment

The end result after you spend hours
doing something

Clear skin

Bad jokes

Colored pens

Being a cool aunt

Any form of praise

Flavored olive oils in your cooking

Putting things back in their place as soon
as you're done with them

A barbecue you don't want to go to
is rained out

Buying exercise clothes
even though you never workout

Diet Stewart's root beer

Low-carb soda

Code words between you and friends

Good karma

Keyless entry to your car

A flapper hat

Peasant tops

The perks unique to your job

Redecorating your place

Getting that answer to the crossword puzzle
you've been agonizing over

A friend whose tastes are totally aligned
with yours

Three week's paid vacation time at work

The maintenance fee of your condo
isn't going up this year

Acting totally out of character once in a while

Silly thoughts you'd never share with anyone

A two-hour lunch when your boss is out of town

Your parents are happily married
after many years

Your garden

Silicone bakewear

A tranquility fountain in your living room

Your birth flower is the calendula (October)

Crochet chic

You can pull off a rich girl's look
on a poor girl's budget

Semi-Homemade Cooking with Sandra Lee
on The Food Network

Being dedicated and determined

Writing your workout sessions
in your planner ahead of time

Belly-dancing for sexy abs

A concealer that can take on any blemish

Crepe makers

Indoor grilling pans

Belgian waffle makers

Crepes with fresh whipped cream

Remembering to renew your registration

Oceanfront hotels

Non-alcoholic beer

Padded satin hangers

Knowing you'd never, ever, ever
date a friend's ex

Wine sans alcohol

Short overalls

Fondue restaurants

A restaurant you love
that never has a long wait

Being seated in a booth

Window seats on an airplane

Preferring fresh fruit to ice cream for dessert

An empty seat next to you on an airplane

The way you used to push your curfew as a teen

Fit magazine

Online friends you'll never meet

A reply to a very important e-mail

Virtual hugs

Renting a bunch of B movies

Forgetting your troubles

A back-up pair of glasses

Southwestern chic

Not being able to fathom how
someone can say she just "forgets to eat"

Desk organizers

Being meticulous to a fault

Patriotic chic

The book sale table at the library

Buying a clothing item you love
in every available color

Shopping alone

Down time after a busy day, week, month

Because air sign chicks
stand up for what they believe in

Working on your tendency
to take things personally

Not being as materialistic as you used to be

Feeling good about your decisions

Lawn seats at a concert

Phone upgrades on your cell plan

Alphabetizing your CD collection

A good laugh when you really need it

Your rainy day fund

Your favorite shampoo is on sale

Nestle Buncha Crunch

The office cutup

Fitting into the next smaller size

A day when your hair comes out just right

Moonlight tours

Your belief in Eastern medicine

A Nathan's hot dog with chili and cheese

A good masseuse

A Home Sweet Home sign on your door

Ouchless hair elastics

Chickpea salad

Your miracle-working dermatologist

Electrolysis

An acupuncturist who makes you feel like new

Double-checking your e-mail for mistakes before sending

Resisting a second piece of cake

Having a skin analysis done

Having a color analysis done

You admit your mistakes

Watching a documentary film

A big star you liked before s/he became big

Having traveled internationally at least once

Knowing where all of your
important documents are

Your company is environmentally conscious

Catching up with an old friend

No fees when you turn in your leased car

Turning your cell phone off
when you just don't want to be reached

Although you wouldn't trade your intelligence
for anything, you sometimes view it as a curse

Quirky friends

The Heartbreak Handbook
by Valerie Frankel and Ellen Tien

VIP treatment

Stopping to pet a dog when you're out walking

A standing date with your girlfriends

An unpleasant task that only took
half as much time as you thought it would

Organic milk in your Starbucks hot chocolate

Knowledgeable workers in stores you frequent

Having an extra day
before going back to work after vacation

Winning Hi-lo on a casino poker machine

Your friends think you're nuts
because it has to be 90°
before you'll turn on the air conditioner

Dotting a lower case "I" with a heart

A delayed opening at work

Settling into a new relationship

Not going over your text messaging limit

Getting out at 3 o'clock
the day of your office holiday party

Clever sayings in greeting cards

Sometimes you'd love to uproot yourself
and start over

Public transportation
that will get you anywhere

In hindsight, things don't look so bad

The piece of mail
you've been eagerly awaiting arrives

Your mom's buttery, homemade pound cake

Bowl-shaped tortilla chips

Not harping on things

Quaint country inns

Treating yourself to a wildflower bouquet

Throwing a surprise party where the
guest of honor is 100 percent surprised

Visiting your old campus during
Homecoming Week

Making a stained glass panel
for one of your small windows

Sharp provolone cheese

Taking a class at the
local computer superstore

A single flower in a bud vase

Scorpio chicks + Virgo men

Baking soda to exfoliate your skin

Making homemade chocolates
on a rainy afternoon

A picnic in the park for one

All of the antioxidants in blueberry juice

Having had your name painted
on the driver's side door of your first car

The last guest doesn't leave your party
till 4 A.M.

Scones on Sunday morning

Checking into your hotel
after a long day in the car

Sitting and daydreaming for a few minutes

Making your all-time favorite recipe

Going to the beach during a sandcastle contest

International music

Playing with tarot cards

A Victoria's Secret clearance catalog

Razors that give a close shave

Your best friend's convertible

Suede pants

Not getting out of Target without spending $100

Knowing the POINTS value of virtually any food

Travel guides

Your fantasies of taking a world cruise

Getting your "I Lost 10 Pounds" ribbon

Equestrian chic

Giving photo CDs as gifts

Your hairdresser opens his own salon

Burning your favorite photos onto CDs

The change of seasons

A canvas field coat in the autumn

Wrinkle-free fabric

Natural beauty tricks

Sleeping off jet lag

Fun, crazy socks

Free drinks while you play the slots

All of the 8 A.M. classes
you sat through hungover

A photo of you that is absolutely fabulous

Choosing a doctoral program

A day with no ringing phone or doorbell

Getting into your first choice MBA program

Ice cream for dinner in the summer

Wearing easy care scrubs to work every day

The great lit you read in your
Women's Literature class in college

Having a much better time than you thought
you would at your high school reunion

Self-publishing

Citrus-scented laundry detergent

Having one of your poems printed in a magazine

Winning a magazine writing contest

Your birth flower is the chrysanthemum
(November)

Chanel sunglasses

The multiple pairs of slouch socks
you wore in junior high school

On-time flights

The loud people seated at the next table
are finished with their meal

Sleeping through a long flight

Putting bookplates
in all of your favorite books

A Bas Bleu catalog

Being seated near the front of the plane
so you can exit quickly

The Museum Store

Dinner cruises

Riverfront hotels

Tandem bicycles

Well-written novels

Pasta in cream sauce

A Tuscan Sangiovese wine

Caesar salad with shrimp

You always save your receipts
in case you want to return something

You're a sucker
for those corny friendship e-mails

Finding the perfect pair of shoes

Baby oil to untangle a necklace

Small boutiques

Beating your deadline

Sidewalk sales

Decorating at The Bombay Company

Reading for pleasure
on your bus or train ride to work

Mentoring a college intern

Sensible Chic on HGTV

Trying an alternative therapy
instead of antibiotics

Umbrella straws

When you were small, it was safe for kids
to run around the neighborhood all day

Going on a double-decker tour bus
in New York City

Wild berry wine coolers

Being able to maintain your weight
without giving it much thought

Your naturally curly hair

Trying skydiving

Being a natural redhead

Fitness cruises

Going for a short walk after dinner

Knowing that your life has a purpose

A new Sarah Brightman CD

Dwelling more on the positive than negative

Sandblasted jeans

Extra virgin olive oil in your cooking

A mini fridge in your office

Unsolved Mysteries segments
followed by updates

Staying within your monthly budget for a change

Newspapers that are written
above a sixth grade reading level

Cocktail-inspired desserts

Movies with endings that aren't predictable

Paperless bills delivered to your e-mailbox

Your Cabbage Patch Kids are somewhere
in the recesses of your parents' attic

Keeping track of your net carbs

Going to the bookstore at midnight
the day a hot release comes out

A friend who always has good stories to tell

Resisting the urge to
completely throw in the towel on your diet

Black and white with bright colors

A zebra print string bikini

Luxe fabrics

A new column in your favorite magazine

Wearing black to a wedding

Not calling into work once
during your vacation

Your mother's beehive hairdo in old photos

A perfectly organized toiletry case

Wine charms

Apple scented candles

Agreeing to disagree with someone
and putting the issue behind you

Sugaring, instead of salting, a cocktail glass

Playing holiday music in October

Baking bread in the autumn

Jane magazine

Taurus chicks + Capricorn men

Sprinkles on your ice cream cone

Going on a moonlight
Jack the Ripper tour in London

Citrus-scented shaving gel

A letter of commendation from your boss
for your professional portfolio

A cute birthmark you have

A leather bookmark from Coach

A cruise to the Mexican Riviera

Being blessed with ample boobs

Cooking with wine

How easy registries make shopping

You never feel like a third wheel
with your best friend and her boyfriend

Superhero movies

You're Invited on The Style Network

Your excellent credit rating

Swimsuits with ample bust support

Visiting your favorite city

When someone takes your suggestion

Watching the Olympics

Looking through your best friend's
wedding album

Throwing yourself a party
when you get a graduate degree

Cheap costume jewelry

Haagen-Dazs

Back-to back songs on the radio
by your favorite artist

No line at the inspection station

Getting that extra hour during
Daylight Savings Time in the fall

Your package arrived

Labor Day weekend

Online package tracking

Everyone ahead of you in line pays with cash

A parking space at the mall
close to the store you're going to

New notebooks at the beginning of the semester

Photo note cards

Non-smoking hotel rooms

Sidesplitting comedies

Getting your paralegal certificate

A copy clerk at your office
who gets the job done ASAP

Completing your student teaching

Horns beeping around your town
on graduation day

Fleetwood Mac's Greatest Hits

Taking the easy way out once in a while

How seriously you took yourself
as a teen/pre-teen

Having an assistant at work

Because you believe the cliché,
"When one door closes, another one opens."

Seeing Faith Hill and Tim McGraw in concert

Recipes with only five or six ingredients

Not being one of those people
incapable of making the smallest decision

Finding yourself talking about characters on TV
shows as if they're real people

Being a sucker for reality dating shows

Going to a baseball game with your dad

Courtside seats at a basketball game

Referring to your apartment
as your "Bachelorette Pad"

Dawson's Creek reruns

Sewing scented sachets for your lingerie chest

Hosting a wine and food pairing dinner

Making your quiches with half and half
instead of heavy cream

Going to your beach house during the week
when no one else is there

Spending an afternoon watching soaps

Quirky expressions you love

Christmas tree shops

Being good to yourself

Not believing everything you hear

The trepidation you feel
right before the roller coaster drops

Jogging clothes with reflector strips

Cherry vanilla margaritas

Your birthstone is opal

Squats

Monthly to-do lists

Online home affordability calculators

Donating old books to a shelter or hospital

Your old sorority T-shirts

Sepia-colored photographs

Spraying your sheets with cologne

Spray body lotion

Wasting time once in a while

Experimenting with spices in your cooking

Dimmer switches for mood lighting

Taking a watercolor painting class

Interesting coffee table books

Last night's pizza for breakfast

Having your carpets cleaned
(by someone else)

The picture hanging on your wall
looks perfectly straight

Photographic essays

Be Late for Something Day (September 5)

A new shopping center

Fake jewel stones on your toes

Funnel cakes

Writing things down so you don't forget them

Having your pet groomed

A trusted pet sitter

Finding out that the bad news you heard
is untrue

Your corner office

Your own parking space at work

Knowing sign language

L.L. Bean flannel-lined jeans

An inconspicuous deodorant check

Practically furnishing your entire first
apartment at Wal-Mart

The courses in college that taught you the most

Seeing someone close to you
successfully battle his or her addiction

A brand new mattress

Spending a morning watching game shows

Your parents' inground pool

Crispy noodles

A glass of wine and a hot tub

Pisces chicks + Cancer men

Terra Chips

Your neighbor signs for a package for you
when you're not home

Going to see the Christmas tree
in Rockefeller Center

Preferring to tell an awkward truth than lie

Your life finally seems to be coming together

A million choices at the candle store

Sequin change purses in holiday shapes

Frozen grapes

Breadsticks with Parmesan and garlic
dipped in marinara

Being gracious in the most awkward situation

Cooking Light magazine

Going to a jazz festival

Heat-activated hair care products

All-day shopping passes

Homemade multigrain pancakes

A root beer float and a hot dog

Champagne brunches

Your friends always come to you
for guy advice

Your sister always comes to you for career advice

The sound of genuine laughter

Gourmet magazine

Raspberry-scented hair removal lotion

Cupcakes with pink buttercream icing

Being invited to your five-year-old niece's
Barbie's wedding

A free gift when you open a bank account

The glittery Tinkerbell T-shirt
you're too old for but bought anyway

A chic apron

Intimate get-togethers

A pasta-making machine in your kitchen

A steaming cup of tea
when you sense a cold coming on

Telling a good guy from a creep

Catalina Island

Using alliteration by accident in your writing

An encyclopedia of letters on your bookshelf

A 10-year/100,000 warranty on your car

Going to a regatta

A spaghetti strap tank
over a short sleeve crew neck tee

Sending cards for Grandparents' Day

International Women's Day (March 8)

Not letting your fears sidetrack you

Getting the patch

Taking a carriage ride in New York City

Being asked to lead a seminar

Terrycloth hats

A Chanel jacket with jeans

Making even the most ordinary day
a special one

Finding shorts
with more than a three-inch inseam

A 500-page novel waiting to be read

Throwing a horror movie party

The Louis Vuitton City Guide

Not being able to stand your cousin's boyfriend, but killing him with kindness anyway

Potato pancakes

Playing a game of tennis

It takes two weeks to get through one day on your soap opera

Going to college on a full scholarship

Making time to do the things you want to

Babying your hair

Warm neutrals

Swim sales

Well-written TV scripts

Your high school boyfriend looks you up

Bustle-back gowns

Neoprene cell phone holders

Remembering to use a coupon before it expires

Silk georgette

Leather flip-flops

The last dish from your dinner party is dried and put away

Screwless wine openers

Ceramic lanterns

A pot of lip gloss

Watches with jelly straps

Getting a $700 dress for $59.95
at an outlet center

Visiting the mansions in Newport, R.I.

Sightseeing in a foreign city

Slimming vertical stripes

A weekend in Washington, D.C.

Low-carb cocktails

Knowing a B.S. story when you hear one

Going to the Fourth of July fireworks
with your girlfriends

Jello shots

Nachos with Cheez Whiz

A friend calls just to say "Hi"

Owning and operating a cordless drill

Owning a complete service for 8 people

Doodling while you're on the phone

A sweater tied around your shoulders

Taking a self-defense course

Acting on a hunch and being right

Pizza that is piping hot when it's delivered

Knowing when to use "good"
and when to use "well"

The short-lived series *Savannah*

Holiday-colored M & Ms

Your Amazon wish list

Candy hearts postage stamps

Cheesy '80s horror movies

Interactive party planners

eBay University classes in your area

Perfect blood pressure at the doctor's office

A facial sauna

Restaurants with bottomless fries

No longer being employed at your menial first job

Outdoorsy chic

They're finally hiring a file clerk at the office

Your younger brother's college graduation

A pool table in your basement

An online quiz to see which Greek goddess
you are most like

Mini trampoline workouts

Believing in fairies

Practicing Aikido

Attending at least one major sporting event

Planning to one day write
the Great American Novel

Having made a total fool of yourself
and recovering

Finding inspiration when you really need it

Performing an anonymous good deed

Being invited to lunch

A great book was recommended to you

The person before you on the copy machine
didn't leave it jammed

Going to bed an hour early

Judy Blume's adult books

A slimming hairstyle

A coffee filter to strain wine
with broken cork in it

Glass bead sunglass chains

Microfiber beach towels

Design on a Dime on HGTV

Reading online diet diaries for inspiration

Finding shortcuts for unpleasant chores

Turning slightly from the camera
for the best result

Plotting your biorhythms

Black and white Hitchcock films

Making a list of things to do before you turn
30 or 40, and actually doing them

Your car didn't get egged on Mischief Night

Gothic romance novels

Purple pens

Dancing to your favorite songs
in the privacy of your own home

Still loving to watch Disney movies

An interesting case when you're on a jury

Taking a cake decorating class

Throwing a '70s disco party

Grilled extra sharp cheddar cheese on rye bread

Believing that ultimately, justice prevails

Adding celery seeds to your cold salads

Knowing there's no accounting for taste

Accessory stores

A bold and outrageous accent piece
in your living room

Serving a simple dish for dinner
that looks like much more work than it was

Pinwheel cocktail picks

You haven't spotted a gray hair yet

Buying a gift that the recipient will love, even if you don't

A weeklong seminar at a culinary school

Beaded tea light holders

Bikini trimmers

Putting together your own gift baskets

Resolving old issues

Deciding to go back to school for an additional degree

Always coordinating bows and ribbons with your wrapping paper

Scheduling a "Do Nothing" day

White capri pants

Having been on two or more continents

Returning a wallet you found

Defragging your computer

Your handy paper shredder

Gourmet-kitchen cooking in your tiny apartment kitchen

Alternative music

A pinstriped suit

Bath confetti

Getting the answer you'd hoped for

No lines at the grocery store

Saving all of the receipts
for your expense report

Patterned cropped pajama bottoms

The first holiday you celebrate
with your new mate

Clean-cut guys

Boardwalk pizza

A 20-minute catnap

Remembering everything you need
at the supermarket

Receiving a handmade gift

Water resistance exercises

Your birth flower is the narcissus (December)

Making your own jack o'lantern for Halloween

Your upcoming vacation to Greece

Crocheting or knitting

Running a 6-minute mile

Having adult furniture in your
apartment/condo/house

The story of your life . . . so far

Bowling a strike

A hands-free phone in your car

Dramatically changing your hairstyle without telling a single soul first

Acing an audition

Pastel-colored steno pads

Being fluent in a language other than English

The time in college when you camped out overnight for concert tickets

Writing a letter to Santa even though you're over the age of ten

Riding a cable car in San Francisco

Your great idea for a funky invention

A kiss on your forehead

De-stressing with a walk through a community garden

Being the victim of a benevolent practical joke

Your dream of retiring before 40

Front-row seats

You work with a bunch of great people

A smile from a baby

Freshly made tortillas at a Tex-Mex restaurant

A long drive ahead of you

"Thunder Road" by Bruce Springsteen

Saving your New Year's resolutions to review
as the year progresses

Sign-on bonuses

Buying your boyfriend
the male version of your perfume

Passing the stage where nice guys turn you off

Sending a thank you note
to the host of a great party

Going with your best friend
to taste test wedding cakes

Visiting the Museum of Natural History

Your real estate taxes
aren't going up (much) this year

Having a regularly scheduled,
annual getaway with your friends

Staying in the shower twice as long as usual

The sound of your girlfriends' laughter
at your boyfriend's jokes

Showing up at your parents' house,
unannounced, at any time, walk right in,
and they'll be thrilled to see you

Finding the perfect slice of pizza